MORE WORLD WAR II AIRCRAFT IN COMBAT

47 FAMOUS WARPLANES DEPICTED IN RAGING CONFLICT

GLENN B. BAVOUSETT

ARCO PUBLISHING, INC.
NEW YORK

Dedication

THIS BOOK IS DEDICATED to Joseph Pokraka, James Howard, Dr. Stanley Ulanoff, David McCampbell, and William Hess, all of whom came to my rescue in my hour of greatest distress. Without their courage and faith, this book may not have been.

Published by Arco Publishing, Inc.
219 Park Avenue South, New York, N.Y. 10003

Copyright © 1981 by Glenn B. Bavousett

Library of Congress Cataloging in Publication Data

Bavousett, Glenn B.
    More World War II aircraft in combat.

    Includes index.
    1. World War, 1939–1945—Aerial operations.
2. Airplanes, Military.   I. Title.
D785.B32   940.54′4   80-12082
ISBN 0-668-04550-7 (Library Edition)
ISBN 0-668-04563-9 (Paper Edition)

Printed in the United States of America

Contents

THE LUFTWAFFE GALLERY—Eagles in the Sky

Acknowledgments

Due to circumstances beyond my control, the record of those who provided input to this effort has been lost, if not destroyed. This is regrettable because it was a sizeable list, too lengthy for me to remember in its entirety, and I did want to acknowledge everyone on it personally.

I do, however, recall some who contributed: The U.S. Navy for information on the *Devastator*; Jun Amper, in the Philippines, for data on the P-26 *Peashooter*; a Californian—I think—for furnishing the *Kingcobra* kit when none could be found; the person who furnished the kit correction data on the *Kingcobra* and Il-2 *Shturmoviki*; a Texan—I think you live in Houston—who sent photos taken in Russia that showed how they modified the *Kingcobra* to add more firepower on the upper forward fuselage; a tank modeler from Fort Worth, who supplied the tank used in the Hs 129 scene; a German, who prefers to remain anonymous, for information on the He 219 *Uhu*; all personnel at the Royal Air Force Museum for their generosities to Les while he was there; the Air Museum in West Germany; the Confederate Air Force; and, finally, three persons who made major contributions, and I will never forget their names: William N. Hess of Houston, Texas; Dr. Stanley M. Ulanoff of Roslyn, New York; and Christopher Shores of London, England.

Of course, there were many others...and I thank each and every one of you.

Foreword

If a painting is worth a thousand words, Glenn B. Bavousett gives us thirty-six thousand words—as a starter.

Here, put into vivid colors and placed on canvas by the deft brush of Tony Weddel, are scenes of World War II aerial combat—combat that brings back memories slowly fading into oblivion for many of us who took part in it.

For those too young to remember, or yet unborn, the paintings are priceless portrayals of engagements fought in a bitter conflict. Through extensive research, attention to detail of battle engagement and airborne equipment, and participant or witness verification, the paintings and their story lines become historical documents that will be cherished more and more as the World War II years fade from living memory.

Though I have personally flown, inspected, or seen most of the aircraft portrayed in this book, my review of the contents found my memory slipping on many of the details. Such things as the color schemes of the Fw 190's and Me 109's of Oberst Josef "Pips" Priller's *Jagdgeschwader*, Number 26, "Schlageter." But well remembered are the flaming spouts that appeared from the forward cowling and leading edges of their wings as mass head-on attacks of these vicious "black-crossed" fighters bore down on us.

They took their toll on us in the early days of 1943. Likewise, by D–Day in June of 1944, we'd clawed and scratched through several score or more of their evasive machines and better pilots.

At the present time, Group Captain Robert Stanford-Tuck, of R.A.F. Fighter fame, and the earlier Kommandant of *Jagdgeschwa-*

7

der 26, Oberst Adolph Galland, couldn't give you the details of their opponents' unit colorations or markings either. In an *augenblick* (blink of an eye), as the Germans say, each could provide a verbal schematic of his opponent's fighting machine, but only as a hazy recollection imprinted in the back of his mind.

Offhand, the various performances of opponents' aircraft have also slipped away. It would take a review of old documents to sharpen the gray matter. Thank goodness someone has recorded these details for posterity.

It would be remiss not to recognize the role of the stalwart pilots and crews of the "Big Friends" that carried the payloads of destruction to the enemy heartland, whether they flew the B-17's or B-24's in daylight raids, or rose to fly east during the hours of darkness in R.A.F. Bomber Command's Halifaxes, Lancasters, or Wellingtons. From our fighter bases located on the East Anglia Coast of England, we often heard the early morning hours of assembly of aerial armadas of the Eighth Air Force. Before first light, the continuous drone of their motors drowned the crow of the rooster. From October until late March the weather over the British Isles became dismally worse. By Christmas the "pea soup" fogs, so notorious in London, settled with an ominous presence over everyone and everything. Blind flying became a hazard in itself.

To marshal a thousand or more bombers into combat wings of fifty-plus four-engine bombers was mind shattering. Between clouds, between layers, or above clouds, the show pressed on. Once a string of combat formations gained altitude and established a course, the aerial array stretched 150 to 200 miles. A spectacular display, to say the least. A still more breathtaking scene occurred when atmospheric conditions at 20,000 feet or more became conducive to the formation of condensation trails. The sky became filled with man-made stratus. For those in the cockpits, it was a harrowing day just to cross into enemy territory.

Adrenalin stimulated faster heartbeats from this point on. Heavy, black flak bursts appeared ahead. Those of us in fighters "ducked" around these menacing "steel hailstorms."

Enemy fighters could be anticipated. They could come in waves, in small gaggles, in coordinated strings from head-on, or in fleeting individual attacks from above. Whether the enemy aircraft concentrated attention on a lead "box of bombs" or moved back to launch attacks upon following combat wings depended upon many a factor: i.e., tactics, directions from ground controllers, cloud cover, visibility, bomber stragglers, escorting fighter protection, etc.

A concerted, concentrated attack on one combat wing was most dreaded. Here the attack overwhelmed the mutual protective coverage of turret gunners. Such coordinated attacks literally blew formations apart as "Big Friends" went down with burning engines, shot-out cockpits, damaged controls, exploding gasoline tanks, and a multitude of other unlisted disasters. The objective of an ideal fighter attack was to launch from the sun with complete surprise into a violent head-on attack at very high speeds. The results were devastating and nerve shattering.

Once a bomber formation began losing members, the attention of the opponent concentrated on the lonely singles that struggled to keep airborne. It was bullet for bullet. Hammer, hammer, hammer! A test of the highest degree of courage.

The Luftwaffe pilot held no position of envy, either. It was necessary for him to concentrate on one target, fly through a hail of bullets, and escape to a safe recovery. Likely as not, this sequence of events had to be repeated several times on the same mission. Not an enviable role.

Having spoken with Luftwaffe Ace George P. Eder, I learned that he destroyed 36 four-engine bombers in his overall credit of 78 aerial victories. Eder was shot down seven times in the course of his flying career, winding up in the hospital with a .50-caliber bullet through his stomach. He still returned to fly again, in combat!

At times, a leisurely, late afternoon jaunt along the perimeter track or to the maintenance hangar cleared the mind for contemplation of the day's work. But the rumble of hundreds of motors could be heard in the surrounding countryside as day's light ebbed. The air battle over Europe seldom ceased whether night or day. The R.A.F. Bomber Command awakened under cover of darkness to carry on the "around the clock" aerial assault.

First off were the Pathfinder forces who dropped flares to light up and designate targets. These swift, two-engine *Mosquitos* swept low over our base as they established climbing speed over the North Sea to altitude and the enemy coast. Further to the east lay a somber vastness of foreboding darkness. A blackout prevailed over the continent, but the complex Luftwaffe system of "Wildschwein" stood on the alert. Thousands of crews manned radar. Night fighter pilots waited their call. Hundreds of flak and searchlight teams readied their stations.

By darkness, heavily laden *Halifaxes*, *Lancasters*, and *Wellingtons* arose from Midland air bases. Except for moonlit nights, when an occasional outline could be discerned, only the rumble of laboring engines were to be heard as the main force passed overhead. With navigation lights turned off, and exhaust manifolds shielded, only the rhythm of synchronized motors prevailed. A thousand or more R.A.F. bombers, flying individually at different altitudes, took over an hour to pass. The stream seemed endless.

Late in the war, as a P.O.W. passing through Berlin, I experienced the devastation wrought by this awesome aerial force. The Berlin sky first opened up with a barrage of anti-aircraft fire that exceeded the imagination. In contrast to daylight, when heavy flak appears as black puffs against the pale blue sky, the explosions of an 88mm shell in the blackness of night comes with a startling flash, followed by a deep rumble. When hundreds of guns are in action, the earth shakes. Shell fragments descending to earth again clatter on rooftops, streets, and sidewalks.

Almost simultaneously, the eerie blackness is broken by target marking flares dropped by the errant *Mosquito* Pathfinder. Dangling from parachutes, the flares light up the surroundings as they slowly descend. A massive explosion follows, which grows in intensity as the big "heavies" unload their destruction. Fires break out; searchlights sweep the sky; the flak barrage continues.

I am escorted into a concrete bunker by my guards, where I crouch as the incessant crash of bombs continues into the night. There is little conversation among those assembled. As an occasional near miss explodes, everyone flinches. A sense of utter helplessness prevails.

How can one describe the actual scene in words alone? Bavousett and his Glenn Illustrators team of artists have caught, with definitive authenticity, instances of rare exposures of the machines and men who clashed so violently. Through these paintings and the synopsized stories which they portray, we are provided glimpses of an era during the late 1930s and early 1940s when people struggled to the death for air supremacy to preserve their respective ways of life. A record and a reminder for future generations.

COLONEL HUB ZEMKE, U.S.A.F. (RETIRED)
Commander, 56th Fighter and 479th
Fighter Groups during portions of WW II

Introduction

Even though I was a deep water sailor during World War II, my first love was combat aircraft. Like legions of other youngsters, I had amassed a great collection of the old solid balsa models and read every printed word about airplanes that could be found. Then, after the war, we all busied ourselves with building futures: The war was now something to talk about occasionally, and the models were set aside. For me the excitement of men and machines tangling in a death struggle in the sky began to fade from memory. Eventually, the whole scene disappeared; it was as though none of it had ever happened. I had forgotten.

Then, in the late 1960's, I had occasion to travel with a close friend to Harlingen, Texas. Dick was going there to be installed as a Colonel in the Confederate Air Force ... whatever that was! In the back of his truck were two metal detectors, the prime reason for my wanting to tag along. After Dick had done this thing with the CAF, we were going to Padre Island and search for the lost Spanish treasures buried under the sandy beaches. Now *that* sounded like a whale of a lot of fun.

But the glamour of the adventure of searching for buried treasure was totally overwhelmed when I came face-to-face with the realities of the mission of the Confederate Air Force. The place was alive with gregarious Colonels and their ladies, and I was seeing the grandest collection of fighting machines in the whole world. Moreover, *all* of them were in flying condition. I was awe-stricken ... speechless. Somebody had cared enough to remember! I *had* to be a part of this assemblage of fine men, all of whom shared at least one common bond: A dedication to the preservation, in flying condition, of at least one of all the more prominent combat aircraft types that had fought in the skies during the 1939–1945 era! Unquestionably, this was a mammoth and awesome task.

This experience gave instant rebirth to my dormant love for WW II combat aircraft. I was neither a pilot nor a mechanic. My value as a crew member was doubtful. But I was an artist and I could write. I began boning up on the old warplanes. I was seeing the real McCoy in the CAF hangars and out on the apron. Unconsciously, a thought was forming in my mind.

In poring through boxes and shelves filled with books covering the great WW II air war, I discovered a near total absence of pictures taken during the combat. There was an abundance of verbal descriptions, the tactics and strategies and all that, but no meaningful photographs of the duelling. The thought became a personal mission for me. If the good Colonels of the CAF could find and restore to flying condition these wonderful combat aircraft, then I could cause them to exist on canvas and depict them in raging battles, the very purpose for which they had been designed and built. By creating combat scenes, I would help these Colonels make the world remember those great pilots from all nations and the mighty machines they flew.

Accordingly, in late 1971, I began the effort that would ultimately emerge as "The Valiant Clan," a collection of 36 canvases that at the time included all of the types of aircraft in the CAF fleet that had seen combat. Because I had searched out stories of battles in which these aircraft participated, the elements for a book were present. In 1976 Arco released this book under the title *World War II Aircraft In Combat*. The book promptly won three awards and became a book club selection.

I began receiving many letters of praise for this work, and nearly all of them asked for more, encouraging me to continue and give similar coverage to other famous combat aircraft. Because of these words of encouragement, and my hopeless love for planes (I admit that I'm hooked!), I pressed on. This companion to the original volume is the result.

The letters I received after the original book was released often posed the question: "Why did you select these particular aircraft?" The answer is, I was essentially tracking those in the CAF fleet. When I decided to commit myself to this companion book, I moved to get as many air enthusiasts involved in the effort as possible. By this time I was selling large lithos of some of the scenes to members of my world-wide "The Valiant Clan Print Club." Using that sizeable mailing list, a questionnaire was developed, asking everyone to name five combat aircraft they would like to see put on canvas, and no fair naming any that had been covered previously. The response was staggering, and, after tallying up everything, it quickly developed that four main groupings existed: German markings, British markings, Japanese markings, and a mixture of markings from other nations.

From these four groups I took the 10 aircraft most often named (adding two of my own choice) and began the research for actions in which each was involved. From this process an individual action was isolated, and from that came the particular configurations, colors, markings and, whenever possible, the background of the scene. We have tried to make them as technically and historically accurate as time and the record would permit. The one exception is the Me-163 *Komet* scene. In Jeff Ethell's book on the *Komet*, he describes this action in great detail, and a reproduction of renowned aviation artist Keith Ferris's painting depicting the "unusual" moment in the action adorns the cover. Both are the result of extensive, in-depth research and as such must be regarded as highly accurate. So, rather than duplicate it, we have fudged to show you these two combatants from the other side.

The one lingering question remains, "*What about the Japanese?*" Well, researching the Rising Sun is a most difficult task. It appears that the historians focused their attention on just about everyone except the Japanese. And while I'm probably very wrong, it seems to me the Japanese have taken the position of "Let's forget the whole thing." Precious little information exists on those planes and their pilots; if it does exist, then it has thus far escaped me. The original plan was to include 12 Japanese planes in this book and leave out the 12 mixed markings. I was making good headway in regard to meaningful stories and the technical information necessary to create excellent scenes when, unfortunately, I was *hors de combat*, so to speak, from mid-1977 to 1979. This put the Japanese on a back burner for more than two years because it was impossible for me then to perform research of this nature. The great Japanese warplanes, and others, will be covered in my next effort of 36 scenes.

What you are about to read and see on the following pages took some four years to complete. The planes are presented to you in the order in which the canvases were created: First the British, then the mixed nationalities, to completion with the Germans. It is hoped the stories and their accompanying scenes will fire your imagination, and cause you to glance back in time to ponder on and remember this great era of our aviation history. It is a legacy passed on to us by those who fought for what they believed was right. In time they will all be gone, taking with them their first-hand accounts of how it was; the dwindling supply of the actual planes will surely follow, to leave only the written word and a few remarkable paintings.

My heartfelt thanks go out to all of the Colonels of the Confederate Air Force, for were it not for these super-dedicated men, not a single scene would have come from me.

GLENN B. BAVOUSETT

THE BRITISH GALLERY

Battlers Courageous

Foreword

True justice for the indomitable British Empire and Commonwealth and Free European pilots and crews, and their aircraft, cannot begin to be exposed by the following twelve stories and their accompanying scenes. At best this gallery only cracks the door to permit a brief glimpse back into a time when these fearless people rose to the occasion, to truly cause "...their finest hour," and this applies across the board and not just to that part of the whole—the Battle of Britain—that triggered Churchill to utter the words.

Several of the combat aircraft covered in the following pages were on-line and ready to fight from day one of the war, and they went on to continue fighting until the last day of the war. Others were born later in the unfolding drama, and some of these would continue to bare their teeth and fight in another place at another time.

Like a good wine, the taste of these aircraft lingers on after the glass is emptied. A picture is still just a picture and, as such, cannot raise the hackle of hair on the neck and back like when coming face-to-face with one of these machines that dedicated people have seen fit to preserve. There is a difference. Quite a number of combat aircraft are on public display in various museums in England and the United States. You are encouraged to see them and feel the thrill of your life as you stand there imagining the smells and sounds of war; the electrifying experience of man and machine locked in mortal combat with another man and his machine. It is difficult not to imagine yourself at the controls, roaring down on the Möhne, hot after Wick, driving a torpedo into the *Littorio*, kicking on rudder to put your guns on a *Falco*, diving down to absolutely pulverize a locomotive. Yes, it is still possible to see yourself ease a wing-tip into position to flip a doodle-bug out of control. That, my friend, is the hawk within you rising to the surface . . . the same hawkishness that put those airmen—men just like you—in these planes and made them do what they had to do. For some it is a nostalgic trip back in time, for others a letdown from being born too late, but for all it is a chance to pause and reflect, ponder and remember, for what goes 'round does come back.

The canvases of these twelve history-rich scenes are now a part of the private collection of Douglas Champlin and can be seen at Falcon Field Fighters Air Museum located in Mesa, Arizona.

And now we present to you *Battlers Courageous*, the name given to The British Gallery by a fan of our work.

Westland *Lysander*

"'Lizzie'—the foot-soldier's friend!" This catch-phrase aptly describes the intended use of this versatile aircraft.

The *Lysander* was designed to conform to outdated specifications developed for army cooperation airplanes, a concept similar to the U.S.A.A.C.'s equally outdated Observation category of aircraft used for front line tasks. In many respects the *Lysander* was very similar to its U.S. and German counterparts—the Curtiss O-52 *Owl* and the Henschel Hs 126.

Operating from rough forward area airstrips, the design criteria called for a multitude of jobs to be performed by the *Lysander*. S.T.O.L. capabilities were high on the list, and Westland engineers satisfied this with the long-span, high-lift wing of unusual plan form that became one of "Lizzie's" most pronounced physical features. As an army cooperation airplane, the *Lysander* was to undertake tactical reconnaissance, direct artillery fire, drop messages, carry urgent supplies to the front line, and carry out limited ground attack duties. For these latter purposes, a .303in Browning machine gun was fixed on each of the heavily-spatted wheel coverings—another distinguishing feature that clearly identified the plane to be a "Lizzie." Additionally, outrigger racks—thin, stubby wings—were fitted to the wheel coverings, and these were used to carry supply containers or small bombs. Further, 40-pound bombs could be carried in a small bomb rack mounted beneath the rear fuselage. Lizzie was not without some teeth!

Seven squadrons of *Lysanders* were available to the R.A.F. in September of 1939. Four of these squadrons accompanied the R.A.F.'s Air Component of the British Expeditionary Force when it went to France. These aircraft formed 50 (Army Cooperation) Wing which was there to provide support for the ground forces. During the

uneventful winter of 1939–40, these four squadrons of *Lysanders* were joined by a fifth, and all of them saw their first action in the opening days of the *blitzkrieg* in May of 1940.

Usually, only a single *Lysander* went up on a tactical reconnaissance flight, but sometimes they would operate in pairs. Regardless of their number, they frequently fell afoul of the Luftwaffe fighters for which they were usually "easy meat." *Lysanders* had their moments of glory, however, when they managed to outfight their attackers. This didn't happen too often, but it did happen!

Sixteen aircraft from 16 Squadron effected the biggest concerted raid by *Lysanders* on record when they attacked a German convoy near Cambrai on May the 15th.

On May 22nd, Flying Officer A.F. Doidge and his gunner, Leading Aircraftsman Webborn of 2 Squadron, were en route to the Merville area to effect a recon mission when they came across a Ju 87B *Stuka* dive-bomber. The enemy was promptly engaged in combat and Webborn made the kill. Doidge then looked ahead and below and saw a plane of his opposite number—a Henschel Hs 126! Doidge immediately dived to attack, and with a burst from his front guns sent the Henschel down in flames to crash and burn.

A more typical *Lysander* situation for this period is depicted in our scene. The date is May the 17th and the time of day is early morning. Pilot Officer C.H. Dearden, also of 2 Squadron, is at the controls and he's in the Cambrai area when he's jumped by no less than nine of those ferocious Messerschmitt Bf 109 fighter planes. Dearden began taking all of the evasive actions possible with his highly maneuverable *Lysander,* and while none of the German pilots managed to send him down in flames, they eventually inflicted enough damage to force him to land. The badly damaged *Lysander* was later burned on the ground to prevent it from falling into German hands.

The last *Lysanders* were evacuated from France on May the 22nd. Then they operated over Amiens, Boulogne, Calais, and Dunkirk, providing support as required to the retreating Allied army. When operations ceased for these aircraft on June the 8th, the five *Lysander* squadrons had lost a total of 30 aircraft.

Lysander crews also saw limited action over the North African deserts, Eritrea, Greece and Madagascar, and against the Japanese in Burma. Her pilots also flew anti-terrorist missions in Palestine and on the North-West frontier of India. Later in the war, "Lizzie" flew out of England and Burma on clandestine night operations to land secret agents in enemy-held territory.

"Lizzie" was a fine and tough Lady!

◀ *Westland Lysander*

Vickers *Wellington*

More Vickers *Wellingtons* were built during World War II than any other British bomber type: 11,000 of them rolled off the production lines. Indeed, only three other bombers were built in greater quantities: the B-17 *Flying Fortress*, B-24 *Liberator*, and Junkers Ju 88. The *Wellington* was destined to remain in service from the first to the last days of the War.

In September of 1939, the "Wimpy" was the R.A.F. Bomber Command's best heavy bomber. The craft was built on Dr. Barnes Wallis's geodetic construction principle which featured a "basketwork" structure of criss-cross light metal framers which were then covered with fabric. This principle required no internal bracing, spars, or stringers, and offered lightweight construction with considerable strength. Since each section of the aircraft was self-supporting, it had the ability to absorb tremendous punishment without crumbling. However, the necessity of cladding the outer surface with fabric, rather than with stressed aluminum, limited its development for flight at higher speeds. Additional speed was the trade-off for being able to take plenty of punishment.

In the early stage of the developing war, it was the consensus of considered opinions of aerial warfare strategists and tacticians that tight formations of heavily armed bombers would be able to penetrate enemy territory without needing any fighter escort, relying instead on the mutual support of their guns for protection against attacking fighter planes. This theory is similar to that espoused by the U.S.A.A.F. when it entered the European war in 1942.

Accordingly, the *Wellington* 1A, which became operational shortly after the hostilities commenced, featured twin machine-gun power turrets in the nose and tail and a retractable "dustbin" turret in the lower fuselage. This "undergunning" would quickly manifest itself for all to see when mutual support failed to be an effective defense against an onslaught by enemy fighters.

A few of these ineffective mutual support missions was all it took for Bomber Command to shift from daylight to night bombing missions. The month of December in 1939 forecast the need to change.

Several daylight raids by *Wellington* formations were launched against units of the German Fleet in the Wilhelmshaven area located on the northern coast of Germany, where the Baltic meets the North Sea. On two occasions the *Wellingtons* suffered bad losses to the guns of German fighters, and then, on the 18th of December, came a colossal disaster.

Twenty-four *Wellingtons* of 9, 37, and 149 Squadrons approached Heligoland on the third daylight raid of the month. A strong force of Messerschmitt Bf 109's and Bf 110's of the composite *Geschwader Schumacher* had been gathered for defense of the area, to handle the very threat that was now approaching. Fully alerted to the menace, the Germans rose from their airfields to intercept the *Wellingtons*. The resulting fight came to be known as "The Battle of the Heligoland Bight" (the subject for our painting) and produced the disaster in which 12 *Wellingtons* were shot down and three others so badly damaged that one ditched during the return flight and the other two crashed when landing.

Further losses in daylight raids over Norway during April of 1940 hammered home the lesson and, thereafter, Bomber Command operated only by night, except in unusual circumstances. While a failure during the daylight hours, the *Wellington* gained great success as a night bomber.

"Wimpy" went on to operate in practically every theater of war in which the illustrious R.A.F. was employed: Over Germany, the African desert, Italy, Burma, and other areas, this great bomber provided the main striking force until at least 1943.

Wellington was the last twin-engined type to be replaced by the newer four-engined "heavies," and it soldiered on much longer than did her other twin-engined compatriots. The craft was also widely used as a torpedo-bomber, an anti-submarine patrol aircraft and, to a lesser extent, for night photo-recon, aerial minesweeping, and transport duties. While never exported, the *Wellington* did serve with the Free European air force within the R.A.F., and was flown by Poles and Czechs.

Boulton-Paul *Defiant*

The *Defiant* was unique inasmuch as it remained the only single-engine, two seat, turret-mounted fighter plane to see action during World War II.

This aircraft was powered by the same 1,000 h.p. Rolls-Royce Merlin engine that was used in the more famous *Spitfire* and *Hurricane* fighters, and the resulting underpower produced a lower all-round performance in regard to combat duties. This was due to the aircraft's greater size and weight when compared to that of the *Spit* and *Hurricane*. The additional size and weight was, of course, brought about by the inclusion of the four-gun power turret and the gunner who operated it.

The *Defiant* was designed specifically to be a bomber destroyer. The theory was that in passing through a bomber formation the turret gunner would be able to continue the attack from many different angles and give a greater duration of fire than a conventional, single-seat fighter which could only fire forward, usually at only one target, during the pass. In this regard the loss of power was not considered to be important. In practice, however, things didn't work out as planned, because the Germans didn't cooperate. They sent fighters along with the bomber formations, and the underpowered *Defiants* became "duck soup" for these pilots. Moreover, once the bombers began to feature heavy armor protection, the battery of four .303in Brownings were no longer particularly effective.

Defiants were first committed to action during the Dunkirk evacuation in May of 1940. Two squadrons of the aircraft were operated as day fighters, and in this role their service was both brief and bloody. *Defiants* were not, however, totally ineffective in combat. Under certain conditions the plane and its crew constituted an awesome adversary that was tough to cope with.

When 264 Squadron made its debut over Dunkirk, its surprise value allowed a few successes to be achieved, for the German fighter pilots mistakenly assumed the *Defiants* were *Hurricanes* and, naturally, employed the classic attack from above and behind...and were promptly greeted with a wall of blistering fire from the fully alerted turret gunners! But this type of attack was quickly changed once the Germans were wise to the *Defiant's* aft-firing capability. Now they attacked from below or head-on, where the gunner could not train the turret, and the slaughter of the underpowered *Defiants* was fearful.

The *Defiant's* moment of glory came in late May of 1940. Early in the day of May the 29th, 264 Squadron mauled a formation of unsuspecting Messerschmitt Bf 110 *Zerstörers*. Later that same day the squadron got in amongst a host of slow and lightly armed Ju 87 *Stukas* and cut them to pieces (our scene). Total claims for the day's action reached 37, but actual Luftwaffe losses were substantially less than this inflated number. What with the gunners whirling about in their turrets, many firing at the same targets, and the pilots looking but not firing themselves, the situation was fraught with opportunities for overclaiming, to a degree approaching that of the gunners in bomber formations—and those gunners were notorious when it came to overclaiming!

Soon after the opening of the Battle of Britain, the *Defiant* was released as a day fighter and relegated to the role of a night fighter. More squadrons were formed for this role, but the *Defiant* had no radar and could not be adequately fitted with it. As a result, the *Defiant*, as a night fighter, became nothing more than a stop-gap, and enjoyed few successes in this role.

Fairey *Swordfish*

In 1940, the Italian Fleet posed a massive threat to the British Royal Navy in the Mediterranean, and to the security of British forces in Egypt, Malta, and Cyprus. By November 1940, however, the main Italian battle fleet still had not been met at sea after nearly six months of war, and the British Mediterranean Fleet was doing much as it wished, with its carrier-borne aircraft attacking Italian bases in the Aegean and in Libya, while its surface ships escorted munitions convoys to Malta and Alexandria and raided Italian convoys.

The September arrival of the new armored Fleet carrier, H.M.S. *Illustrious*, allowed a strike—Operation Judgement—to be planned against the main Italian Fleet based at Taranto in southern Italy. Operation Judgement was to be a two carrier operation, but at the last moment *Eagle* became unserviceable, due to her fuel lines being damaged by concussion from frequent near-misses by marauding Italian bombers.

Then in early November came news that all six Italian battleships were in the harbor—the attack had to be made at once! *Illustrious's* striking force was not large: She carried eighteen Fairey *Swordfish* torpedo-bombers of the 815 and 819 Squadrons, with the fifteen Fairey *Fulmar* fighters of the 806 Squadron for defense. Four more *Swordfish* and two Sea Gladiator fighters from *Eagle's* 813 Squadron were flown aboard and the carrier, with the battleships, cruisers, and destroyers of the Fleet, headed for the target.

The Fleet was spotted and bombed by the Italians well ahead of the attack, yet the Italian Fleet remained at anchor, taking few extra precautions to get ready for the approaching British—an unforgiveable error in judgment which was to prove costly to Italy.

Although reliable, docile, and highly maneuverable, for which reasons it would remain in service throughout the war, the elderly *Swordfish*—the "Stringbag," as it was affectionately known—was a biplane of relatively low performance. As a consequence, a day strike against the Italians was considered potentially too costly to succeed against so well-defended a major target, particularly without the advantage of surprise. Consequently, a night attack was planned. Accordingly, during the hours of darkness of 11-12 November 1940, the first strike of 12 *Swordfish* went off, six with torpedoes, six with flares and 250-pound S.A.P. bombs. In the face of heavy anti-aircraft fire and a balloon barrage, the torpedo-carriers swept in low, getting in two telling strikes on the battleship *Littorio*, and a third which failed to explode. Another torpedo struck the *Conte di Cavour*, and she sank in shallow waters. One *Swordfish* failed to return.

An hour later, a second strike of five torpedo-carriers and three flare/bomb droppers went in and scored another torpedo hit on the *Littorio* while others hit the *Caio Duilio*, which had to be beached in a sinking condition. Meanwhile, the bombers of the two waves had hit the seaplane base with great accuracy, wrecking it, setting fire to oil storage tanks, and hitting other warships. One more *Swordfish* was lost.

For the loss of two aircraft, the crew of one of which survived to become prisoners of war, the Royal Navy had put half the Italian battle fleet out of action. *Conte di Cavour* was subsequently raised, but never returned to service. *Littorio* and *Caio Duilio* were out of service for over six months. The rest of the Italian Fleet was promptly withdrawn to northern bases, and seldom put to sea again when British aircraft carriers were known to be operating. It was a staggering victory—both material-wise and morale-wise—at a time when the British needed just such a success. It was also the first successful major strike by carrier-based aircraft on an opposing fleet. It is believed by many that the results of Operation Judgement formed the blueprint for the Japanese to refer to when developing their attack plans on the American Fleet at Pearl Harbor.

About two months after the stunning success over the Italian Fleet, *Illustrious* limped across the Atlantic for major repairs in a U.S. shipyard, smashed almost to destruction by German dive-bombers. Such are the fortunes of war!

Supermarine *Spitfire*

It was the general intention of the R.A.F. during the Battle of Britain that the more numerous Hawker *Hurricanes* should concentrate their attention on the German bomber stream while the high-performing Supermarine *Spitfire* should engage the escorting Messerschmitt Bf 109E fighters at high altitude. While in practice this was not always possible, the plan nevertheless worked well most of the time, and the remarkably evenly matched *Spitfires* and Messerschmitts fought many savage duels in the sub-stratosphere over southern England.

By November of 1940, the daylight phase of the Battle was basically at an end, with the bombers now braving the resilient British defense only at night. Nonetheless, the German *Jagdfliger* (fighter pilots) still continued to come over at great height during the daylight hours, either escorting a few "nuisance" fighter-bombers, or on *Freiejagd* (free chase) sweeps that were designed specifically to entice the British fighters up to give battle, and to inflict continuing losses upon them.

Most of the German pilots had been in action almost constantly ever since the previous May 10th, and their scores were mounting. Three men were ahead of all the rest: Majors Werner Mölders, Adolf Galland, and Helmuth Wick, each of whom had been promoted to command a full *Jagdgeschwader* of some 70–100 fighters. By late November of 1940, all three had attained their 50th victories.

After trailing the leaders, Wick pushed into first place when he scored his 55th kill during the morning of November the 28th. Wick reappeared in the British skies that afternoon to seek out additional

31

victims. And, after a further victory, he saw a formation of 12 *Spitfires* below him: This was 609 Squadron, which was one of the most successful Fighter Command units of the Battle.

Six Hundred Nine Squadron had been in the thick of the fighting ever since the evacuation at Dunkirk in late May. This almost constant involvement in the air war resulted in the pilots becoming extremely experienced in combat, especially against the Bf 109 pilots. Leading the British formation was Squadron Leader Michael Robinson, himself an ace, who was to ultimately claim 19½ victories.

Flying one of the other *Spitfires* was Flight Commander Fl. Lt. John Dundas, who, at the time, was the squadron's top scorer with 12½ victories. Dundas had been a pre-war, "part-time" Auxilliary pilot. He was an urbane, sophisticated, and highly educated man as well as an intellectual and gifted sportsman. Dundas was a very popular person.

Upon spotting the unsuspecting *Spitfires*, Wick, a dedicated professional airman, led his *Schwarme* of four Messerschmitts down to attack, but was seen in the nick of time to allow the break to be called by Robinson.

Wick caught a *Spit* in his sights, fired, and saw his rounds slamming into it. Dundas was on Wick's tail at once and began firing, causing mortal damage to the Messerschmitt (which is our scene recording *When Aces Meet*). "Whoopee! I've got a one-oh-nine!" Dundas enthused to the others. "Good show, John!" Robinson shot back, and even as he spoke Dundas's *Spitfire*, and that of his wingman, P.O. Ballion, were catching rounds that sent them plummeting to follow after Wick's machine. The three bailed out of their stricken aircraft near the Isle of Wight, off the southern coast of England, and while blossomed parachutes were seen, neither Dundas nor Wick were ever found; only Ballion survived the combat.

One of the victors in this melee was Lieutenant Rudi Pflanz, Wick's Number 2. Pflanz was already an ace when he participated in the engagement. He was a tough pilot and would have certainly claimed his 52nd victory on the Western Front had he not met his death in combat—with *Spitfires*—in July of 1942.

And so it went!

Gloster *Gladiator*

As a contemporary of the U.S. Navy's Grumman F3F fighter family, the Gloster *Gladiator* was one of the last classic biplane fighters.

This plane was to be immortalized in the story of *Faith, Hope, and Charity*, which were the names of a trio of Gloster *Gladiators* that were supposed to have defended the island of Malta when they rose into the sky to do battle with hordes of attacking Italian bombers. To a great extent this thrilling story was a piece of brilliant wartime propaganda designed for home island consumption, for the fact was the achievements of the *Gladiators* stationed on Malta were very limited. At the time, enemy raids on the island were quite infrequent. Moreover, the defenses were soon reinforced by tidy numbers of the more potent *Hurricane* fighter planes. Despite this, the *Gladiator* did earn its place in aviation's "Hall of Fame."

In October of 1939, at the beginning of World War II, this spiffy little fighter plane was still operational in Britain and France. One can only imagine the gut-wrenching feelings of her pilots once they became knowledgeable of the awesome fighting capabilities of the power-laden Messerschmitt Bf 109's: Chariots pitted against tanks! Well, it had happened before.

Gladiator pilots fought the hard fight over Norway in 1940, operating some of the time from the surface of a frozen lake. It was in the Mediterranean theater, however, where the *Gladiator* was to truly make its mark: not so much in the skies over Malta, as the story went, but over Greece and in the parched sky above the sun-baked desert of North Africa, where the sturdy plane provided the R.A.F.'s sole fighter equipment during the beginning months of the war, holding the line until its bigger, more sophisticated fighter cousins could arrive. *Gladiators* also flew from the heaving decks of Royal Navy aircraft carriers to provide air defense for the Mediterranean Fleet during the summer of 1940, a task the plane performed with great success.

The obsolete fighter was always outclassed by the German machines; her pilots ached to become embroiled in an even match, to test once and for all time the mettle of the machine and pilot...and they knew there was probably only one place on the planet where the test could be made—in the sky above the Western Desert of North Africa. If the *Gladiator* was to leave its mark, then it would be here.

On 8 August 1940, 14 *Gladiators* of 80 Squadron, R.A.F., lifted up from the desert sands to form up and fly an early evening sweep over Italian territory.

They were not alone in the desert sky.

A flight of 16 Fiat CR-42 *Falcos*, also biplane fighters, from the 9 and 10 *Gruppo* of the 4 *Stormo C.T.* of the *Regia Aeronautica* were flying cover for Meridionali Ro 37bis reconnaissance biplanes on a mission to the front line.

The two opposing forces met in the area of El Gobi near the frontier between Egypt and Libya, and the well-matched formations clashed violently. The long awaited test was on!

This, then, had to be *the* air battle for us to capture and record on canvas. Because it represents a milestone, perhaps the very last one in the history of the biplane fighter as a combatant, we have recorded the action from two viewpoints and corresponding paintings. The "sister" scene to this one appears later in the book when we cover the *Falco*.

Back to the battle near El Gobi.

When the raging, twisting, and turning fight was over, and the dust and smoke had cleared, seven of the Italian fighters had gone down, against an R.A.F. claim for nine kills and six probables. This against 80 Squadron's own loss of two *Gladiators*. The mark had been left!

Among the successful R.A.F. pilots, several of whom were destined to become future aces, was Flight Lieutenant M.T. Pattle, who would later be considered as the probable top-scorer in the R.A.F. Pattle is believed to have raised his total victories to 50 before his untimely death in Greece in 1941.

The R.A.F. was not the only user of *Gladiators*. Other air forces also employed the plane: South Africa, Norway, Finland, Belgium, and Greece. The fighter was also seen in the China skies during that nation's struggle with the Japanese in the late 1930's. *Gladiators* also served peacefully with the air forces of Latvia, Portugal, Egypt, Eire, and Sweden. This last nation actually sent a volunteer unit armed with *Gladiators* to aid the Finns in their winter war with the Soviet Union late in 1939.

The *Gladiator* was indeed a true international fighter.

Bristol *Beaufighter*

The *Beaufighter* was developed from the *Beaufort* torpedo-bomber. It was a big, heavy aircraft—one of the largest and heaviest twin-engined fighters to see service during World War II.

The plane was not particularly fast or maneuverable, but it was sturdy, reliable and, best of all, packed a terrific punch, with four 20mm cannons in the nose and six .303 machine guns in the wings, mounted (oddly) four in one wing and two in the other! The *Beau's* very size provided one of its secrets for being able to wreak massive damage on just about any target trapped in the gun-sight. The radar operator/navigator, who was seated well back in the capacious fuselage, could reload the cannons while in flight—a unique advantage for a WW II fighter plane!

Because of its size, the *Beaufighter* was able to carry the first airborne radar sets, which were both bulky and unwieldy. Therefore, the plane's first combat role upon entering service was that of a night fighter and, as such, the *Beau* became the most effective element in England's defense during the terrible *blitz* in the winter of 1940–1941. Then, as production increased, radarless *Beaufighters* began operating as long-range day fighters. The *Beau's* first job in this capacity was with the R.A.F.'s Coastal Command, with whom the assignment was to hunt and destroy German anti-shipping bombers snooping for targets around the coasts of Britain and in the Bay of Biscay. The *Beau* was, however, soon sent to the Mediterranean, where she was to first operate out of Malta with the assignment to use her guns to disrupt the Axis communications network, which stretched from southern Europe to the North African coast.

Following the Anglo-American landings in French North Africa in 1942, the *Beaufighters* of 272 Squadron, flying from the island of Malta, played great havoc with the stream of Axis transport aircraft on ferry missions across the Mediterranean from Sicily to Tripoli or Tunis. One of the highlights of this period—and it is the subject of our painting—occurred on 24 November 1942, when the Australian *Beaufighter* ace, Flying Officer "Ern" Coate, shot down a giant six-engined Blohm and Voss Bv 222 flying boat. His victim was one of the prototypes of this aircraft that had been pressed into service for the emergency, and was Coate's fifth victory of a final total of 9½.

Then, operating from airfields in the desert, *Beaus* struck at Axis airfields, convoys, and other targets of opportunity, inflicting great punishment on the enemy wherever he was found. Night fighter configurations quickly joined the day fighters to counter the enemy's night bombing raids on Suez and Malta...at every turn the enemy seemed to be met by a *Beaufighter* of one kind or another!

And it was not long after the initial Japanese assault on Burma in early 1942 that *Beaufighters* arrived at bases in India. From here the mighty *Beaus* went out by day to strafe the long and tortuous Japanese lines of communication in Burma and then to provide night defense for Indian cities such as Calcutta.

Under license, Australia built a sizeable quantity of *Beaufighters* and employed them in operations—mainly in the anti-shipping role— around the islands of the South-West Pacific. It was here they flew alongside the aircraft of General Kenney's 5th Air Force in the never-ending quest to relentlessly beat back the enemy.

As the war progressed, *Beaufighters* were adapted to effectively perform other combat roles dictated by new tactics brought about by the ever-changing face of war. This included being first loaded with bombs, then rockets, then torpedoes. Because of her adaptability, the *Beau* remained in action to the very end of the hostilities.

The versatile *Beaufighter* was even supplied under reverse Lend-Lease to several U.S.A.A.F. squadrons operating out of Italy. The Americans were quick to use them for many jobs—as both day and night fighters, against shipping in the Adriatic, and in support of Tito's partisans in Yugoslavia. And the *Beau* continued her anti-shipping role back home by flying with the Coastal Command's Strike Wings around the coasts of North-West Europe and Norway.

Avro *Lancaster*

Until the first atomic bomb was detonated, the dream of many inventors of WW II weapons was to devise a weapon that, with a single blow, would effectively shorten the war.

One such attempt was made by the brilliant innovator and aircraft designer, Dr. Barnes Wallis, after he laid a curious eye toward the German Ruhr. Four mighty dams spanned the Ruhr: the Möhne, Eder, Sorpe, and Enneppe, and each held back tons upon tons of water used to supply hydroelectric power to Ruhr Valley industry. Wallis reasoned that if these dams were broken, the resulting flood would not only be devastating to those caught in the Ruhr at the time, but would also cause a disastrous loss of prime power, vital to the war industry located there. Certainly! Break the dams and the war would be shortened.

Now the question "How to do it?" formed in Wallis's active mind. He knew that for every problem there is at least one answer. He knew conventional aerial bombardment was out of the question: Waves of bomber formations would be required, and the losses to enemy flak and fighters would not be worth the results to be gained. Neither would it do to send in planes carrying super-powerful torpedoes: The crafty Germans had already covered themselves by spreading torpedo nets in front of the dams. There was only one practical way to do it, and that was to skip a powerful bomb across the water, using the same principle small boys employ to skim flat stones across a pond or stream. Bounce the bomb to end its momentum against the dam, next to which it would sink and then explode, and the dam would break! A devastating flood would follow.

First, a weapon was needed. Wallis devised a large cylinder packed with RDX high explosive. The brute he built weighed in at nearly 10,000 pounds!

Then, the weapon carrier. Not much of a choice here. It could be carried only by the four-engined Avro *Lancaster* bomber, the greatest load-carrier of the war. Accordingly, specially-modified bombers were delivered to a newly-formed unit—the 617 Squadron—which was destined to go down in history as The Dambusters!

Now came the resolution of the variables: At what height and distance do we launch the weapon to cause the cylinder to bounce and stop next to the dam? Through trial and error all of this was worked out to perfection, but not before some ingeniously simple devices were created to overcome the inadequacy of flight instruments available at the time.

Again, the bomb. The rascal wouldn't behave the same way each time it was launched. This erratic performance was tamed when it was discovered that it would track a true path, bouncing a constant number of times en route to playing out, when it was released, spinning, at 500 r.p.m.

The next problem was the distance for release. Releasing too early or too late would result in a good try only, for any damage inflicted under either of these conditions would be negligible. The distance problem was solved by mathematics and a very simple optical device. The distance between the two fixed parapets on the dam was known. A simple instrument having two pencil-sized uprights, spaced apart mathematically, was made for use by the bombardier. The instrument was positioned before the bombardier's eyes at a mathematically pre-determined distance. When the run-to-target began, the two uprights would be seen on either side of the parapets, and they would then move toward the parapets as the bomber closed in on the dam. The launch point came when the uprights overlayed the parapets.

Then, the exact height necessary to cause the right number of bounces was calculated. This was to be an extremely low bomb run, and as such it had to have error-free execution. Powerful spotlights were mounted under the nose and tail and then trained downward at pre-determined angles that caused the beams to cross each other at the exact distance to get the proper bombing height. The two spotlights would be turned on when the run-to-target commenced and an observer would monitor the two spots on the water's surface. As the pilot lowered the altitude, the two spots would naturally move toward each other, and the correct altitude was attained when they converged. The observer would, of course, be in continuous contact with all members of the crew as he called out the movement of the spots.

After several weeks of extensive and highly secret training, the mission was launched during the night of 16–17 May 1943. Nineteen *Lancasters* rose and formed up in three waves of three groups each and flew out low over the sea to escape detection by enemy radar. The first force of nine bombers was led by the commanding officer, Wing Commander Guy Gibson, a veteran bomber pilot, whose target assignment was the biggest dam—the Möhne. Gibson would bomb first when they arrived at the target. The big bomber came roaring over the lake a scant 60 feet above its calm surface; Gibson's speed, 220 m.p.h. The altitude lights popped on, and upon seeing them the Germans on the dam opened up at point-blank range laying down concentrated light automatic flak. Gibson pressed on, the observer feeding altitude inputs, the bombardier's eyes frozen to his sights. It was a perfect run-to-target with the beams and sights converging when and as they should. The bombardier depressed the bomb release button and the spinning cylinder-bomb fell away to strike the water and begin bouncing (our scene) to mate perfectly with and explode against the dam.

But the Möhne held, and failed to break!

The next on-rushing bomber was hit by flak, breaking the precision required for a perfect launch, and the bomb bounced to hit a parapet and explode without causing any serious damage. (We can only imagine the emotional state of mind present in the Germans manning those light automatics!)

The third attacking *Lancaster* dropped short, but the next two in were spot on target and with a mighty roar the concrete and masonry of the dam crumbled, sending a great jet of pent-up water thundering into the valley below.

The Möhne had been broken!

But not without the British paying a price: One of Gibson's *Lancs* was lost to flak on the way in. Now Gibson led the remaining still-armed *Lancasters* to the Eder Dam. The first *Lancaster's* run-to-target was too low and it struck a parapet and was destroyed from the blast of its own bomb. The next two, however, made letter-perfect releases and the Eder, too, was split asunder.

A host of problems consumed the other two formations, each of which were composed of five *Lancasters*. One could not find its target and returned home with the bomb intact; two had returned early after suffering heavy flak damage; four others went down. The three remaining *Lancasters* attacked the Sorpe Dam and failed to break it, then the Enneppe Dam without effect. One more *Lancaster*, flown by deputy commander Sqn. Ldr. H.M. Young, was lost on the return flight over Holland. In all, seven of the 19 *Lancasters* failed to return.

The damage was extensive. Ruhr coal mines, power stations, and factories up to 40 miles away were flooded. Communications were disrupted and hundreds of people were drowned, but the results to the German war industry were far less devastating than had been hoped for, and the dams were subsequently repaired. A repeat attack could not be made, for the necessary defensive measures involving steel nets, increased flak, balloon barges, and smoke screens were quickly and efficiently instituted by the Germans.

Wing Commander Gibson, who received the Victoria Cross for his leadership of this daring attack, is seen in our painting, which captures the moment after the bomb was launched. Months later, after completing several tours both as a bomber and night fighter pilot, Gibson was assigned to a staff post. He managed to beg for "just one more raid, this time in a light *Mosquito*"; Gibson did not return.

Handley-Page *Halifax*

While overshadowed by its famous compatriot, the *Lancaster*, the *Halifax* preceded the latter's entry into service with the R.A.F.'s Bomber Command by several months.

Halifaxes were the second British four-engined bomber to be ordered in quantity, and they made their first operational sorties during 1941. The *Halifax* rapidly became the second most important British bomber in terms of numbers, for no less than 6,176 of these big aircraft were to be built.

The bomber was steadily developed and improved, and the later versions to enter service bore little resemblance to the early production models. Powered variously with Merlin in-line engines or Bristol Hercules radials, the *Halifax*, in its several models, flew in excess of 82,000 sorties with Bomber Command, and during these sorties suffered 1,833 operational losses. Her bombardiers did, however, drop nearly a quarter of a million Imperial tons of bombs on the enemy.

Thirty-four Squadrons of Bomber Command were to use the *Halifax* during the war over Europe. Two of these squadrons were units of the French *Armee de l'Air* which had been attached to the R.A.F. By the latter part of the war the bomber was being used mainly by No. 4 Group and the all-Canadian No. 6 Group, with the former flying large number of *Halifax* Mark B.VI's and the latter Mark B.VII's. During June of 1944, the *Halifax*-equipped No. 4 Group achieved the Command's best success rate of the war when the Group's gunners claimed 33 intercepting night fighters shot down that month.

44

Other *Halifaxes* served in the Mediterranean from 1942 to 1944. Here they raided targets in Libya, Tunisia, Crete, Sicily, Italy, and the Balkans. More served with Coastal Command, functioning as long range anti-submarine patrol bombers which went out to sweep the vast wastes of the Atlantic.

The great majority of the *Halifax's* work was undertaken at night during 1943–44, but by the end of the latter year the virtual disappearance of the Luftwaffe from in the skies over Western Europe allowed the bombers to begin making large-scale daylight attacks, similar to those being flown by the U.S. 8th Air Force. When this change from night to day occurred, wings of R.A.F. *Mustang* fighters were formed to give escort and provide protection to the relatively lightly armed British "heavies."

Accordingly, interceptions by the Germans were indeed rare. Exceptions did occur, however, when on odd occasions some of the formidable new Messerschmitt Me 262 jet fighters would appear out of nowhere and manage to break through the fighter escort to rip into the bomber formation. It is this duelling between *Halifaxes* and Me 262's that we selected to record with a painting.

Hawker *Tempest*

In 1940 the Hawker *Hurricane* was one of the heroes of the Battle of Britain, but by then it was already past its prime. Sidney Camm, the designer of this famous fighter, set out to produce a new high performance interceptor designed around a massive new 2,000 h.p. engine. The result was the *Typhoon*, a powerful monster, dragged along at over 400 m.p.h. by the 24-cylinder Napier Sabre engine. Yet, while the *Typhoon* would later become one of the finest fighter-bombers of the war, as an interceptor the aircraft quickly proved to be a flop!

Wind tunnel tests soon showed the reason for the *Typhoon's* lack of performance at high altitude—Camm's wing design had closely followed that of the *Hurricane* and was far too thick in section, producing the unacceptable levels of drag above certain altitudes. Back on the drawing board, Camm refined his design with an elegant, ultra-thin wing of elliptical planform, which he married to a cleaned-up fuselage and larger tail surface. The result was the *Tempest*, a superlative fighting machine that was put into production with all possible speed.

Featuring high speed, good maneuverability, a heavy armament of four 20mm cannons buried in its graceful wings, together with massive power for the climb and adequate weight for the dive, the *Tempest* was unequalled as a low and medium altitude fighter during the last year of the war in Europe.

This new fighter entered service in the spring of 1944 and had its first taste of combat during the Normandy invasion. Within a matter of days, however, all available *Tempest* units were pulled back to

combat the deadly V-1 "doodle-bugs" that were then appearing over southern England. The *Tempest* proved to be one of the few fighters able to catch the bombs in level flight, and thus became their main executioners. Squadron Leader Joseph Berry, top scorer against the bombs, with 60 of them shot down, gained all of his successes while flying the *Tempest*, as did many of the other leading "bomb-busters."

At the end of September 1944, with the worst of the threat from the V-1's past, the *Tempest* was released to again operate over the front lines, and five squadrons joined the 2nd Tactical Air Force in Holland and Belgium. The *Tempests* were very active in the fighting over the Ardennes during the famous Battle of the Bulge in late 1944, but had their heyday during the spring of 1945. In a useful partnership with the high-altitude, Griffon-engined *Spitfire* XIV's, they hunted the dwindling Luftwaffe throughout northern Germany, exacting a heavy toll each time the enemy came up to fight. Throughout the final seven months of the war, the *Tempests* were employed purely as air superiority fighters, patrolling in the areas where they were most likely to bring the Luftwaffe up to do battle, and haunting the airfields from which the Luftwaffe's jet-powered Messerschmitt Me 262's were operating. In the process, they claimed the honors as being the R.A.F.'s best killer of these formidable new opponents. When the war ended in May of 1945, *Tempest* strength in Europe had been increased to seven squadrons.

One of the greatest exponents of the fighter was New Zealander Evan Mackie, who ended the war leading the largest *Tempest* Wing. Mackie gained the last 5½ of his 21½ victories flying these aircraft, and also used it in destroying other German planes on the ground. But his combat on 7 March 1945 was remembered by him as his hardest of the war. In a twisting, turning fight with a "long-nose" Focke-Wulf Fw 190D, Mackie was literally bathed in sweat before he managed to finally put a burst into the enemy fighter at maximum deflection, sending it blazing down to crash and explode. It was Mackie's 19th victory, and it is this epic combat that is recorded in our scene. At the time, Mackie was commanding 80 Squadron—one of the R.A.F's top-scoring units of the war.

◀ *Hawker Tempest*

Hawker *Typhoon*

"Never enough time to do it right, but always enough time to do it over!" This age-old adage was surely uttered on more than one occasion in regard to the *Typhoon*, for here was an aircraft, designed as an interceptor for use by the R.A.F., that was nothing but a heap of trouble when it first entered service in 1942.

The root of the *Typhoon's* problems formed when it was rushed into production before the airframe had been fully proved and the new and tempermental 2,000 h.p. Napier Sabre 24-cylinder in-line engine had been fully readied for service. As the result, the plane showed a disappointing performance at higher altitudes where the official design called for it to operate. Moreover, the premature introduction into service caused a spate of nerve-shattering accidents to occur: Either the tail would break off, or the engine caught on fire, seized up, or leaked poisonous fumes into the cockpit! For a time it looked as though the *Typhoon* would have to be withdrawn.

It was the Germans and not necessarily the British who gave a second chance to the *Typhoon*. The reprieve came in early 1943 when Focke-Wulf Fw 190 fighter-bombers began a series of low-level hit-and-run raids on the southern coast of England. The *Typhoon* was pressed into service to interrupt this menace and quickly proved it was the one aircraft in the R.A.F.'s inventory that could catch the raiders at this height. It was now clear that the *Typhoon* was no good as a high altitude fighter, but at low levels it more than held its own with the best the Luftwaffe could pit against it.

Accordingly, Hawker strengthened the tail surface, then attacked the plane's many other maladies to correct them gradually, but the Sabre engine always had to be treated with care.

50

Then, in 1943, an entirely new and promising future opened up for the *Typhoon*, when bombs were fitted beneath the wings to try her as a fighter-bomber. The *Typhoon* reached the pinnacle of success in this classic combination when, later in the year, launching rails to accommodate eight of the new 3-inch rocket projectiles were fitted beneath the wings. This muscular arsenal, coupled with the existing armament of four 20mm cannons, gave the *Typhoon* enormous hitting power.

In the months prior to the invasion of Normandy, *Typhoon* fighter-bombers swept the coasts of France and Belgium, bombing and rocketing and strafing radar stations, knocking out bridges, mangling rail targets, airfields, and coastal defenses, shooting up convoys and other like targets, completely terrorizing the enemy at every turn.

When the invasion was launched in 1944, *Typhoons* were among the first aircraft to be moved onto airstrips within the beachhead. Eighteen squadrons of these deadly aircraft provided the R.A.F.'s main, close support strength. And they were active from the onset, quickly establishing their position as oppressors of the German Panzer Divisions.

Throughout the remainder of the war, the *Typhoons* brought their awesome firepower to bear on the Germans: Breaking up armored attacks, winkling out 88mm guns, *Nebelwerfer* multi-barrel mortars, self-propelled guns, Tiger tanks, and other strong points holding up the Allied infantry or tanks during the offensives, playing havoc with the German columns at Falaise, and generally creating mayhem. When the front was quiet, they ranged behind the German lines on interdiction missions, hunting transport columns, rail locomotives, barges, and other river traffic which were attacked with cannon, rockets, and bombs.

Although not employed on any other front, the *Typhoon* was without any doubt *the* British fighter-bomber of the war.

Gloster *Meteor*

The Gloster *Meteor I* was the first Allied jet-powered aircraft to see combat duty during World War II.

It was less of a great leap forward in aeronautical progress than was the first production jet, the Messerschmitt Me 262. The *Meteor's* performance and armament was similar to that of late war, piston-engined fighters. Nonetheless, the *Meteor* pointed the way to the many advances in the state-of-the-art made possible by the jet engine.

Meteors were pressed into service with the R.A.F.'s 616 Squadron during the summer of 1944, when the Anglo-American forces were struggling to establish their beachheads in Normandy. Initially, the new jet fighter was employed only to intercept and destroy the V-1 flying bombs that were raining down on southern England at the time. The *Meteor* proved to be one of the few aircraft capable of catching the "buzz bombs," or "doodle-bugs," as the British were prone to call them, in level flight. Normally, the *Meteor* pilot would select his target, give chase to close in, and shoot it down. Occasionally, a pilot would, for one reason or another, fly right up to the doodle-bug and maneuver a wing-tip to below the bomb's stubby horizontal wing, then flip it (the subject of our painting). This threw the bomb's guidance system out of control and the bloody thing would then crash and explode harmlessly.

It was not until late in 1944 that a few of these aircraft were moved to join R.A.F. units stationed in Holland. Their combat assignment in this rear area was to provide defense against Luftwaffe attacks, should any occur. None ever materialized.

54

Then, in the spring of 1945, when the war was in its final agonies, *Meteors* were released for operations over the front lines. By this time, of course, the once mighty Luftwaffe had been decimated, and it was for this reason that the *Meteor* pilots were to never engage German aircraft in combat in the sky. They did, however, manage to strafe a few on the ground.

Shortly before V-E Day, further squadrons of improved *Meteor Mark III's*, along with other squadrons flying the new DeHavilland *Vampire* jets, were ready for action, and they would have undoubtedly played a major role in the air war had the hostilities lasted longer.

The *Meteor* was, however, destined to see aerial combat. The chance came during the conflict in Korea, where Australian pilots flying the much-developed *Meteor Mark VIII's* did battle with the Russian MIG's. Other *Meteors* also saw limited action in the Middle East, where they were operated by both Egypt and Israel.

THE MIXED GALLERY

Moments of Glory

Foreword

Now come twelve electrifying scenes, each depicting the markings of a mixture of six nationalities locked in mortal combat—Russia, Poland, France, Italy, the Philippines, and the United States—all of which tend to spice up this volume of *More World War II Aircraft in Combat.*

It is on these following pages where you will get a glimpse of combat aircraft that is rarely seen in books, and never before seen in battle. It becomes a thrilling experience to move back in time and sit behind these pilots, to look over their shoulders and see what they saw...you can almost hear the engines growling, feel the plane vibrating beneath you, shuddering with the blasting of the guns, the winds of war whistling past you when your gull-winged P.Z.L. P-11 dives into a formation of Dorniers, as you scream down on the deck in a *King* to rip into German armor, twisting and turning in *Ding Hao!* as you defend *Fortresses* under attack by Bf 110's and 109's. Ah yes...it sets the adrenalin to pumping, this fighting in the sky. Would you dare pit the guns of your obsolete little *Peashooter* against those of the deadly *Zeroes* and *Nells?* Lt. Jesus Villamor and his small band of courageous Filipino pilots did...and scored!

The mighty air arms of the Germans, British, and Americans tend to overshadow those of other countries, whose pilots and planes made their contributions, brief-lived as they may have been. Their duels in the sky have a way of getting lost and forgotten among the countless number of more famous air battles. The *Mustangs* and Bf 109's and *Spitfires* have claimed center stage, shoving aside these no less gallant warriors, who rose to fight and have their moment of glory.

Now let's read about and see twelve such *Moments of Glory*, the original canvases of which are part of the Douglas Champlin private collection on display at the Falcon Field Fighter Air Museum in Mesa, Arizona.

Northrop P-61 *Black Widow*

The Northrop P-61 *Black Widow* was a latecomer to the ETO. The big, twin-engined night fighter still had difficulties to overcome following its arrival in England. The night fighter crews of the 422nd Night Fighter Squadron of the 9th Air Force had to almost give up their planes and, instead, used British-built DeHavilland *Mosquitoes.*

Lt. Colonel O.B. Johnson, commander of the 422nd Squadron, had other ideas for his unit. The *Black Widows* were stripped of the big power turret atop the fuselage and all other excess weight. In this "stripped down" configuration, the aircraft was pitted against the saucy R.A.F. *Mosquito.* In what had been an anxiously awaited competition between the two machines, the big P-61 really showed her stuff. The *Black Widow* proved to be faster than the *Mosquito* at altitudes from 5,000 to 20,000 feet, easily out-turned the British craft, and left it wanting in rate-of-climb tests. The men of the 422nd were ready for a taste of combat.

The *Black Widows* began their scoring after their arrival in France in August of 1944. The determination and perserverance of the crews of the 422nd knew no bounds, for once directed to a German intruder by the ground controller, the radar observer tracked down his prey on his primitive radar scope, steadily closing on the target until the pilot could bring the aircraft in position to shoot it from the sky.

While flying a defensive patrol over Belgium during the night of 4 October 1944, radar observer Lt. Robert A. Tierney picked up a contact three miles out and at an altitude of 21,500 feet. Under Tierney's guidance, the pilot of the *Black Widow*, Lt. Paul A. Smith, followed the enemy plane through its mild evasive action up to an altitude of 24,000 feet, where visual contact was made.

61

Smith pulled "Lady Gen" up to within 400 feet directly astern and slightly below the positively identified Messerschmitt 410. After one short burst and one long burst, strikes were observed on the fuselage and wings, followed by a small flash, then a large explosion as the target dropped off on his back, debris falling off and thick smoke pouring from both engines. The Messerschmitt was then observed in a vertical dive which culminated in a violent explosion when it crashed into the ground.

Smith and Tierney went on to become the first of three "ace" crews of the 422nd Night Fighter Squadron. By the time the war ended in Europe, the P-61's of the unit had destroyed 43 enemy aircraft in the air to become the most successful A.A.F. night fighter squadron of World War II. The *Black Widows* of the 422nd scored victories ranging from airspeeds of 375 indicated at 24,000 feet (against the Messerschmitt downed by Smith and Tierney) to a Junkers Ju 52 which was shot down at 90 IAS at 1,000 feet. In addition to enemy aircraft, the unit was also credited with five V-1 flying bombs, numerous locomotives, rolling stock, and ground installations.

The lethal Northrop fighter left a little-known but nonetheless indelible mark in the history of night fighter operations during World War II.

Brewster F2A-3 *Buffalo*

The Japanese forces were riding high in the spring of 1942. They had taken Malaya, the Philippines, Wake Island, Guam, and had suffered what they considered to be only a temporary reversal at the Battle of the Coral Sea.

Japanese Admiral Isoroku Yamamoto knew that he must make a move to draw the American fleet out into a battle so it could be destroyed once and for all. To accomplish this, he sent a feigning task force toward the Aleutian Islands off Alaska, while his main force steamed toward the American base at Midway Island.

Three lethal Japanese forces set out for the tiny island: An occupation force of troop transports, escorted by a light carrier, battleships, cruisers, and destroyers; a main striking force, built around four large carriers; and the third force, which consisted of battleships, cruisers, and destroyers.

The Americans had one very important initial advantage: The breaking of the Japanese cipher code enabled them to learn of the impending attack, and thus divert all of their meager forces toward Midway.

While the United States fleet sped to meet the rapidly approaching enemy force, the pitiful garrison on Midway girded themselves for the coming battle. The primary island defense lay in the hands of the one and only fighter squadron based on that scant piece of real estate: United Stated Marine Corps VMF-221, under the command of Major Floyd B. Parks. The unit was equipped primarily with 20 outdated Brewster F2A-3 *Buffaloes*. The original model of the aircraft had performed well; it was maneuverable, carried four .50-caliber

machine guns, and was a stable firing platform. Subsequent modifications had, however, increased its weight to the point that its maneuverability had become poor and its rate of climb pathetic.

VMF-221's brief moment of glory came on the morning of 4 June 1942, when a U.S. Navy patrol bomber sighted the first task force of the Japanese fleet approaching Midway. Major Parks led a force of seven *Buffaloes* and five Grumman F4F *Wildcats* out to intercept a formation of enemy aircraft that had been launched from the task force and was reported "heading directly for Midway." A second flight of seven *Buffaloes* and one *Wildcat*, under the leadership of Captain Kirk Armistead, were vectored ten miles out to await possible action coming from another direction.

The fighter pilots with Parks were 30 miles out and at an altitude of 14,000 feet when they sighted many enemy *Val* dive bombers 2,000 feet below them and, below the bombers, their screening fighters. The Japanese were so confident of finding Midway asleep that they planned to use the *Zero* fighters only for strafing; hence, the lower altitude.

The *Buffaloes* peeled off and went down after the dive bombers. Several of the enemy craft fell to the Brewsters, but their moment of triumph was short-lived. Once they passed through the tight vee formation of bombers, they were set upon instantly by the escorting *Zeroes*. One after the other the *Buffaloes* were either shot down or cut to ribbons by the Japanese fighters. Even when the fight was joined by Captain Armistead's forces, the Marines still suffered their worst defeat of World War II.

The Japanese lost a few of their aircraft to the *Buffalo* pilots during this fight, but when the combat was over and the Americans counted their losses, 13 of the Brewster *Buffaloes* and two of the *Wildcats* were missing. Of the few that were able to limp back to Midway, only two were airworthy, and neither of these were Brewsters.

The Battle of Midway was a resounding triumph for the U.S. Navy and proved to be the stroke that broke the back of the Japanese fleet, but it was the darkest hour that the men of the Marine Corps fighters had ever known. The qualities their aircraft lacked for their initial combat was made up for by the sheer guts of the pilots of VMF-221. Speaking of the loss of his leader, Major Parks, and all the others on that day, Captain Philip R. White stated: "It is my belief that any commander who orders pilots out for combat in an F2A should consider the pilot as lost before leaving the ground."

Boeing P-26A *Peashooter*

Boeing's P-26A was the last of the U.S. Army Air Corps *Peashooters*. Its predecessors during the late 1920's and early 1930's had all been biplanes, so the arrival of the P-26 on the scene in 1934 made it the pride of the service.

The stub-winged little craft was the first all-metal monoplane fighter accepted by the Army Air Corps. Initial assignment was made to the 20th Pursuit Group at Barksdale Field, Louisiana, the 17th Pursuit Group at March Field, California, and to the 1st Pursuit Group at Selfridge Field, Michigan. The performance and maneuverability of the P-26's made these units the envy of all the pursuit pilots in the Air Corps. The 500 horsepower Pratt and Whitney R-1340 engine propelled the craft along at 211 miles per hour top speed at sea level and achieved a maximum speed of 324 miles per hour at an altitude of 6,000 feet. It was armed with two .30-caliber machine guns that were mounted internally in the fuselage and fired through the propeller.

When war broke out in Europe in 1939, the colorful P-26A's were in the process of being relegated to units outside the United States. A number of the aircraft were assigned to the Panama Canal Zone, to Wheeler Field at Hawaii, and 35 were sent to units in the Philippine Islands.

When war clouds began to gather in the Pacific, last minute attempts were made to build up fighter forces in the Philippines. As the newly designated Army Air Force units began to receive Curtiss P-40's, some of the now very obsolete little P-26's began to trickle into the 6th Pursuit Squadron of the Philippine Army Air Corps. This unit was equipped with nine of the aircraft when the Japanese attacked the Philippines in December of 1941.

The plane that had been the pride of them all in the mid-1930's was in no way capable of taking on the modern aircraft of the Japanese forces, but for the valiant pursuit pilots of the Philippine Army Air Corps there was nothing else available. When Zablan Field came under attack by enemy aircraft on 10 December 1941, Captain Jesus Villamor led a little force of P-26's from Batangas Field to intercept them. While the scrappy Filipino fighters did not down any of the enemy aircraft, they did interrupt the attack and prevented further damage to Zablan.

To have their forces intercepted by such an antiquated enemy was more that the Japanese could stand. On 12 December 1941, 27 Mitsubishi *Nell* bombers, escorted by *Zero* fighters, mounted an attack on Batangas Field. However, when the enemy bombers arrived, a force of five P-26's under the able leadership of Captain Villamor was already airborne and waiting for them.

The *Peashooters* were able to make one diving pass at the Japanese bombers before they were set upon by the escorting *Zeroes*. Villamor sent one of the *Nells* spiraling down before he had to begin the fight of his life against the enemy fighters. Then Lt. Antonio Mondigo's P-26 came under fire and the damage inflicted was so heavy that he had to bail out. When the chute blossomed, Mondigo was set upon by enemy fighters. Lt. Godofredo M. Juliano raced over to rescue his close friend by taunting the *Zero* pilots to come after his *Peashooter*. About this time, Lt. Cesar Basa, who was returning from a recon flight, was swept into the action and shot down.

The 6th Pursuit Squadron paid a heavy price for the one *Nell* that Villamor shot down. But their scrappiness and willingness to fight scattered the Japanese bomber formation, and the tough Filipino pilots gained at least another moral victory for themselves, their people, and the free world.

This action between the *Peashooters* and *Nell* bombers and *Zero* fighters would be the last concerted effort of the Boeing P-26 during World War II, and it was something of a miracle that the last *Peashooter* should be able to leave a mark of victory in a conflict that was so far removed from its original design. The little plane actually claimed a *Zero* a few days later.

Bell P-63 *Kingcobra*

Although the Bell P-63 *Kingcobra* showed a marked resemblance to the Bell P-39 *Airacobra*, the two aircraft were, in fact, two entirely different designs. The *Kingcobra* utilized a laminar flow wing, was a larger aircraft overall, and incorporated the 1,325 horsepower Allison V-1710-93 engine. Armament was composed of a 37mm cannon firing through the propeller hub, two fuselage-mounted, .50-caliber machine guns, and one .50-caliber machine gun mounted in a pod under each wing. Outboard racks under each wing were provided for carrying a 500-pound bomb, and either a fuel drop-tank or another 500-pound bomb could be carried beneath the fuselage.

The heavily armed *Kingcobra* was not lacking in aerial performance, either. The production model—the P-63-A—had a top speed of 410 miles per hour at 25,000 feet and the ability to climb to that altitude in 7.3 minutes. Later models powered with the Allison V-1710-117 engine had a war emergency rating of 1,500 horsepower at sea level and 1,800 horsepower utilizing water injection.

Unfortunately, the *Kingcobra's* entrance into service with the U.S. Army Air Force came at a bad time. When production models became available in October of 1943, the P-47, P-38, and P-51 pretty well had all the fighter plane assignments under control.

Of the 3,308 *Kingcobras* built, 2,421 were destined for delivery to the Soviet Union under the Lend-Lease program. While in service with the Russians, the *Kingcobra* won great acclaim as a ground support aircraft. Its heavy armament and ability to absorb punishment and still come home made the plane a great favorite among the Russian pilots.

70

The *Kingcobras* arrived in the Soviet Union just in time to participate in the spring and summer offenses by the Russians in 1944. During this period the *Kings* played a vital role in helping to contain, if not drive back, German ground forces in the Ukraine. The Russian-flown *Kings* would swoop down on the enemy armor, the pilots holding down the gunners by strafing with cannon and machine guns blazing as they selected juicy targets to go after with the bombs. Then, circling back low on the deck, the pilots would continue to add confusion and destruction to the mayhem by attacking until their ammo was exhausted. Relentless assaults such as this left significant gaps in the German defenses, and the Russian ground forces were quick to advance and exploit the situation to its fullest measure.

We have depicted the *Kingcobra* in the type of operation that made it famous: down on the deck, striking with all its fury at German armor. Untold numbers of German tanks met their fate on the wide expanses of Russia when the Russian pilots came roaring in on them to do battle using the formidable Bell attacker.

Some 300 *Kingcobras* were sent to the French forces in North Africa, but none of them saw combat duty during World War II (actually, they were not uncrated and assembled until after the war was over!). The U.S. Army Air Force did take delivery of 332 P-63's which were utilized in fighter transition programs and in aerial gunnery training.

P.Z.L. P-11

When World War II broke out in September of 1939, and the mighty Luftwaffe appeared in the skies over Poland, the first line fighter force of the Polish Air Force consisted of 128 P.Z.L. P-11 aircraft.

The little gull-winged fighter was originally a design going back to 1931 when the first prototype flew. Delivery of the P-11a to the Polish Air Force began in 1934, and a further development, the P-11b, was built for export to Roumania. The P-11c, which was to see service during World War II, began to enter service in 1935. This version of the aircraft was powered by a P.Z.L.-built Bristol Mercury nine-cylinder radial engine which developed 645 horsepower. The sleek-lined monoplane had a maximum speed of 242 miles per hour at 18,000 feet. It was armed with two 7.7mm machine guns mounted in the fuselage. Some later models incorporated two additional 7.7mm guns mounted in the wings.

The P.Z.L. was an excellent machine in the mid-1930's, but against the Luftwaffe of 1939 it was hopelessly outclassed. Its speed and rate of climb were not sufficient to combat even the German bombers, let alone the power-packed Messerschmitt fighters.

What the Poles lacked in equipment they made up for in intestinal fortitude, for when the bomber formations made their appearance over Poland on 1 September 1939, the little P.Z.L. P-11 fighters were in the thick of the fighting. *The first air victory of World War II was scored by Lt. W. Gnys of the 2nd Polish Air Regiment when he shot down a Junkers Ju 87 dive bomber at 0520 hours on the first day of the war.*

The man who was to become the leading Polish fighter ace of World War II did his initial scoring the following day. This was Stanislaw Skalski of the No. 142 "Wild Ducks" Squadron, who shot down two Dornier Do-17 bombers as his initial victories.

The P.Z.L. fighters fought until practically all of them had been destroyed in combat. Of the 126 confirmed victories scored by the Polish fighter force, practically all were claimed by P.Z.L. pilots. A number of these pilots managed to fly their aircraft to Roumania at the end of the Polish campaign. From Roumania, many of them made their way to France and England, where they continued their battle against the German Luftwaffe.

Douglas TBD *Devastator*

Preliminary action to the Battle of the Coral Sea on 8 May 1942 included some surprises, miscalculations, and over-expenditures of ammunition.

Prior to the big battle, the Japanese pulled a surprise move at Tulagi, a small island 18 miles off Guadalcanal. Admiral Shima's Tulagi invasion group made an unopposed landing May 3rd on the beaches that the U.S. Marines had to win back three months later. (Of the 500 Japanese troops on the island, the Marines buried 427.)

In support of Shima, Admiral Goto's covering group milled about south of New Georgia while Admiral Marushige's support force was sailing some 60 miles farther west. Meanwhile, Admiral Takagi's big carriers, which would eventually tangle with American flattops, were well north of Bougainville, planning to enter the Coral Sea from the east. The real Japanese thrust, the Port Moresby invasion group, destined for New Guinea, was being made ready at Rabaul.

On the morning of May the 3rd, Admirals Fletcher and Fitch, aboard the U.S.S. *Yorktown* and *Lexington*, respectively, were about 100 miles apart and fueling some 500 miles south of Tulagi. At 7:00 P.M. that evening, Jack Fletcher received the report that Australian-based planes had sighted two transports debarking troops off Tulagi, and that five or six Japanese warships were in the area. The American Admiral headed north immediately, determined to strike Tulagi.

Meanwhile, Goto and Marushige were retiring, feeling the island was now secured. Following their easy conquests of the Netherland East Indies, the Japanese expected no counter-attack at Tulagi.

75

Fletcher maintained his 27-knot clip northward through the night and at dawn, May 4th, launched 12 TBD *Devastator* torpedo planes and 28 SBD *Dauntless* dive bombers. Six F4F-3 *Wildcat* fighters performed combat air patrol over the carrier.

Yorktown's attackers were made up of the TBD's of VT-5 and the SBD's of VB-5 and VS-5.

The VS scouting squadron arrived first over Tulagi and began attacking at 8:15 A.M. It dropped thirteen 1,000-pound bombs, damaging the destroyer *Kikuzuki* and sinking two small minesweepers. The torpedo planes came in five minutes later, launching eleven torpedoes but only knocking off the sweeper *Tama Maru*. At 8:30, VB-5 bombers dropped fifteen 1,000 pounders, with possible minor damage to two ships. All planes were back safely on the *Yorktown* by 9:30.

An hour later, the second strike combined 27 SBD's, each carrying a half-ton bomb, and eleven TBD's. The *Daunts* damaged a patrol craft and destroyed two seaplanes. The *Devastators* went through heavy AA fire, and while all were launched, none of the torpedoes hit targets. One plane was lost upon return.

A third attack, at 2:00 P.M., consisted of 21 SBD's which dropped 21 more half-tonners, sinking only four landing barges. That same afternoon, four *Wildcats* were sent up to knock out the three Japanese seaplanes still anchored in Tulagi harbor. They also spotted the destroyer *Yuzuki* and strafed her with four runs, killing the captain and many crewmen, but the ship got away.

By 4:30 P.M. the Battle of Tulagi was over. What stood out was the over-estimation of the Japanese force and the damage inflicted. A Fleet minelayer was taken to be a light cruiser, the transport for a seaplane tender, the larger minesweepers for transports, and landing barges for gunboats; only the two destroyers were correctly identified. The fliers believed they had sunk two destroyers, one freighter, and four gunboats, forced a light cruiser ashore, and damaged a third destroyer, a second freighter, and a seaplane tender.

Also, the attack proved that much was left to be desired in the field of targeting. They had expended 22 torpedoes, seventy-six 1,000-pound bombs, and about 83,000 rounds of machine gun bullets. Admiral Nimitz is reported to have said: "The Tulagi operation was certainly disappointing in terms of ammunition expended to results obtained," and he re-emphasized "... the necessity for target practice at every opportunity."

Lavochkin La-7

The early days of World War II on the Eastern Front saw the Russian Air Force all but driven from the skies by the German Luftwaffe. The Russians had been caught with inferior aircraft and poorly trained pilots. Once the initial onslaught had been overcome, the Russian designers and manufacturers set in motion a massive production campaign that never wavered.

Initially, the men of the Red Air Force had to depend on small quantities of British- and American-built fighters to hold the line until they had sufficient numbers of fighters of their own design. Their pilots received extensive combat training in tactics, and elite units, such as the Russian Guards Regiment, were formed.

One of the more successful designers was Semyon Lavochkin. His Lagg-3 fighter saw action against the Finns in 1941, but its performance there was not particularly outstanding. In late 1941, he took the Lagg-3 airframe and adapted it to take a Shevtosov fourteen-cylinder radial engine. Its performance with this engine was an immediate success. The plane was not only some 25 m.p.h. faster than the Messerschmitt Bf 109F at low altitude, but its low altitude performance enabled it to turn inside the Messerschmitt at will. It was put into production immediately as the La-5 and promptly won considerable fame in its combat against the Luftwaffe.

The last of the Lavochkin designs to see extensive action was the La-7. This aircraft was a refinement of the La-5, with a more powerful engine and three 20mm cannons for armament, rather than the two carried on the La-5. This aircraft was flown by a number of the top Russian fighter aces including Ivan Kozhedub and Alexander Pokryshin.

Ivan Kozhedub was flying his La-7 on a lone reconnaissance patrol on the morning of 15 February 1945, when his eye caught a glimpse of movement over the snow-covered landscape. Then, when the object passed over a bit of woodland and its light gray color betrayed it to be an enemy Messerschmitt M2 262 jet fighter, Kozhedub dived immediately and closed to within 400 yards before the German sighted him. The jet pilot slammed his throttle forward immediately, but by then it was too late: The 20mm cannon shells from the La-7 hammered into the port wing of the German jet and the engine began streaming smoke and flame. Kozhedub fired again, and the 262 went down, cutting a fiery swath in the woods before exploding in a great sheet of flame.

The Red Air Force and its succession of high performance fighter planes, such as the La-7, had proved itself to be as good as any aircraft to see combat in the days of World War II.

North American P-51-B
Mustang

The daylight bombing campaign of the U.S. Army Air Force reached a climax in the fall of 1943. Without having fighter escort to go with them to targets deep in Germany, there was no way that the heavy bombers could continue without taking prohibitive losses. But, at long last, help was on the way.

The North American P-51 fighter possessed the sleek lines of a real thoroughbred and showed promise of living up to its namesake—*Mustang*—even though it suffered, performance-wise, at high altitudes. Through the concerted efforts of Major Tommy Hitchcock of the U.S. Army Air Force, and the Royal Air Force, one of the most fortuitous marriages of World War II was consummated when the P-51 aircraft was mated to the Rolls-Royce Merlin engine. The resulting performance of the aircraft forced the U.S. Army Air Force to sit up and take notice, and the plane was ordered in quantity, with the Packard Motor Company building the Merlin under contract.

The 354th "Pioneer Mustang" Group of the 9th Air Force got into action flying the P-51-B in December of 1943. Although the pilots of the group had not flown the *Mustang* before their arrival in England only a few weeks prior to their first mission, their success was immediate and sensational. Not only were the *Mustangs* able to go all the way to the target with the bombers; the aircraft also proved instantly to be superior to anything the Luftwaffe could put in the air against it. From 20 December 1943, when the 354th scored its first aerial victories, it never looked back. A continuous success was to be theirs throughout their war-time history.

82

The 354th was assigned the task of escorting the heavy bombers to the twin targets of Halberstadt and Oschersleben, Germany, on 11 January 1944. Leading the group was a veteran fighter ace, Major James H. Howard, who had been bloodied in combat while flying over China with the American Volunteer Group, better known as the "Flying Tigers." Howard had taught his pilots well, but on this occasion they were a bit too eager. When enemy fighters were sighted, the flights began breaking off to attack, and the next thing Major Howard knew, he was alone.

Scanning the skies, Howard sighted a bomber formation that was obviously under heavy attack. Without hesitation, he turned his *Mustang "Ding Hao!"* into the fray. For the next half hour he turned in one of the most fantastic performances recorded in the skies over Europe. Time after time, he broke up enemy fighter attacks which had concentrated on the 401st Bombardment Group. The crews of this unit couldn't begin to sing high enough praises for this fighter pilot upon their return to base. They would confirm six victories for him alone.

The modest Howard would only say that he had a "good day" and claimed two confirmed. However, when all the reports were in, everyone concerned took a different view. Major James H. Howard was awarded the Congressional Medal of Honor.

The P-51's would take the bombers to Berlin many times, and to all the other targets that lay deep in Germany where the Luftwaffe had dominated the skies. By the summer of 1944, the *Mustangs* ruled these skies, and before the end of World War II the heavy bombers were able to penetrate the Third Reich at will.

Macchi C. 202 *Folgore*

Undoubtedly the finest fighter to enter combat with the Italian *Regia Aeronautica* during World War II was the Macchi C. 202. This sleek-lined aircraft was powered with an in-line, liquid cooled Daimler-Benz engine which was built under license in Italy as the Alfa Romeo R.A. 100 R.C. 41.

From its initial flight on 10 August 1940, the *Folgore* (Lightning) proved to be a real thoroughbred. Maximum speed was 375 miles per hour at 18,370 feet and the rate of climb was excellent and its maneuverability was superb. Armament was composed of two 12.7mm machine guns firing through the propeller and two 7.7mm machine guns mounted in the wings.

The Macchi C. 202 was initially assigned to units of No. 1 *Stormo* in the summer of 1941. By November of that year the units were in action in Libya. During 1942 the *Folgores* of No. 1 *Stormo* and No. 4 *Stormo* saw extensive action not only against the Royal Air Force in North Africa but also in the skies over the island of Malta. In the course of these air battles the Macchi C. 202 enjoyed considerable success against the first line fighters of the Royal Air Force. The aircraft could turn easily inside the Curtiss *Tomahawks* and *Kittyhawks* and the Hawker *Hurricanes*, and managed to hold its own against the vaunted *Spitfires*.

An Italian ace, whose star began to rise while flying the Macchi C. 202 during the summer and fall of 1942, was *Capitano* Franco Bordoni-Bisleri. Seven of his twelve victories in North Africa were scored during the brief period between October the 20th to November the 7th. His most outstanding feat was the downing of two Curtiss *Kittyhawks* in a wild dogfight on 1 November 1942.

On this day, twelve *Kittyhawks* of No. 250 Squadron, Royal Air Force, had set out to strafe the Mersa Matruh road when they were jumped by four MC 202's of 18 Gruppo. During a ten minute dogfight, three of the *Kittyhawks* fell victim to the Italian *Folgore's* guns, two of them from Bordoni's.

The Macchi C. 202 continued to see action not only against the Royal Air Force but also against the U.S. Army Air Force, which entered the fight in North Africa in November of 1942. In these combats the *Folgore* enjoyed advantages of maneuverability and rate of climb against the P-38 *Lightning*, while the Bell P-39 *Airacobra* was no match whatsoever.

In September of 1942, a detachment of Macchi C. 202's was sent to Russia to operate with No. 21 *Gruppo*. While they were few in number, the *Folgores* gave a very good account of themselves against the Russian *Yaks* and Laggs.

The last of the Macchi C. 202's saw action against the massive Allied air attacks against Sicily and, later, following the invasion of Italy. When the Italians surrendered in 1943, a few Macchi C. 202's served with the R.S.I. Co-Belligerent Air Force in the north of Italy.

Dewoitine D. 520

Had the French *Armee de l'Air* been actively involved in the air war against Germany, no doubt the Dewoitine D. 520 would have attained a degree of fame comparable to the leading fighter planes of World War II.

The design was the brainchild of Emile Dewoitine and his chief designer, Robert Castello. The trim little monoplane was powered by the Hispano-Suiza 12Y21 twelve-cylinder in-line engine, and made its maiden flight on 2 October 1938. The initial flight was a bit disappointing because a maximum speed of only 300 miles per hour was reached, but a modification program upgraded its performance greatly.

The second prototype flew on 28 January 1939, and was a vast improvement over its predecessor. An engine change to the 12Y31 raised the top speed up to 341 miles per hour. The airplane's rate of climb was excellent and the maneuverability was exceptional.

A first production order in April of 1939 called for the manufacture of 200 D. 520's, to be delivered between September and December of that year. War clouds gathering over Europe prompted a subsequent order for 600 more of the aircraft.

France was at war when the first production aircraft rolled off the assembly line. The first true production machine was significantly different from the prototypes. It was powered by an H.S. 12Y45 engine which was equipped with a supercharger and an electric propeller. The armament package consisted of a 20mm cannon, mounted between the engine cylinder banks, which fired through the propeller hub, and four 7.5mm machine guns, two of which fired through the propeller and the other two from their mountings in the wings.

When the German *blitzkrieg* into France and the Low Countries began in May of 1940, only *Groupe de Chasse* I/3 was equipped with the D. 520. Before the Franco-German armistice on 25 June 1940, GC III/3, GC III/6, and GC II/7 were equipped with the Dewoitine fighter. The extraordinary performance of the aircraft is substantiated by the fact that the limited number of units equipped with the D. 520 accounted for 114 confirmed victories and 39 probables. This feat becomes all the more exceptional when it is considered that delivery of the aircraft was made under dire combat circumstances and that pilots had practically no time to train in them.

After the fall of France, a number of Dewoitine D. 520's escaped to North Africa where they became a part of the Vichy Air Force, which operated under the control of the German Armistice Control Commission. Under these controls, production of the Dewoitine was resumed in France and quite a number of French units were furnished with the aircraft.

The Dewoitine D. 520 saw further action against the Royal Air Force in the Mediterranean and also in Syria during June–July of 1941. When the Americans invaded North Africa in November of 1942, both the U.S. Navy and the U.S. Army Air Force encountered and engaged in combat with the testy little French fighter.

The Germans dissolved the French Air Force in November of 1942, but the Dewoitine 520 continued to be produced for use by the Luftwaffe until the summer of 1944. These D. 520's saw duty as training aircraft in Germany right up until the end of hostilities in 1945.

One of the top French aces of World War II flew the D. 520 with great success. Adjutant Pierre Le Gloan was a member of a flight of two aircraft from GC III/6 that engaged a formation of Italian Fiat CR 42 fighters during the afternoon of 15 June 1940. Le Gloan shot down three of the Italian fighters and Captaine Assolant claimed another before they were called upon to return to their base, which was under attack by Italian aircraft. Engaging this force, Le Gloan shot down another CR 42, and then proceeded to claim a reconnaissance Fiat BR 20 before landing. His five victories in one combat brought him an immediate promotion.

Le Gloan was to score 22 victories, primarily in the D. 520, before his death in 1943 in a flying accident.

Dewoitine D. 520

Ilyushin Il-2 *Shturmoviki*

On the morning of 22 June 1941, Hitler's Panzer legions rolled into the Soviet Union. Following the lightning successes of the war in the West that had seen German forces quickly overrun the Netherlands, Belgium, and France, there was immediate speculation that the Russians could not hold out until winter.

Fortunately, it was an early and severe Russian winter that halted the German *blitzkrieg* within sight of the Kremlin spires of Moscow. The war came to a halt until the snow melted, and when it did, the ground turned into a quagmire of mud in the spring of 1942.

Slowly and methodically, the German war machine advanced once more, only to grind to a halt in the southern Ukraine at the city of Stalingrad. Initially, the Soviet Air Force as well as the Russian ground forces had reeled and retreated before the Panzer onslaught, but as new equipment became available the complexion of battle in the sky as well as on the ground began to change.

The most significant challenge to the Germans from the Soviet Air Force came in the form of the most heavily armored, ground attack aircraft that would appear in World War II; the Ilyushin Il-2 *Shturmoviki*. The basic design of the aircraft was extraordinary. The forward fuselage surrounding the engine and the pilot was comprised of an armored shell which ranged in thickness from 5mm to 12mm. Armament consisted of two 7.62 machine guns, two 20mm cannons, and rails for eight 82mm rockets.

Initially the aircraft had been single place, but to further protect the pilot the armored tub was elongated and a gunner armed with a 12.7mm machine gun was added. Progressively, the 20mm cannon in the wings gave way to more powerful 37mm cannon. The awesome machine became known to the German Army as *Schwarz Tod* or "Black Death."

The *Shturmoviki* met with immediate success against the German ground columns and even more so as a tank destroyer. Its cannon and rockets took a tremendous toll of armored equipment. Although an unwieldy-looking machine, its low altitude attack capability and its armor made the aircraft a formidable opponent against Luftwaffe fighter planes. The early Il-2 had only two weak points which were vulnerable to its opponents; the oil cooler under the fuselage and the wooden empennage. With the arrival of the two-seat version of the Il-2, with its armored shield for the oil cooler, only one point of weakness was left, leaving beam fighter attacks from either side at low altitude most troublesome.

On 20 November 1942, the Russian Army opened a great counter-attack against the German forces in the southern salient of the Stalingrad front. Poor weather made air support difficult, but the Il-2 pilots continued to make life miserable for the enemy. On November 21st, Hero of the Soviet Union Captain V. M. Golubev, led his six Il-2s against a German airfield in the area. Despite heavy flak, the Russian fliers silenced the anti-aircraft guns and destroyed eight German aircraft on the ground.

On the return home the Russians encountered Messerschmitt 109's flown by pilots of the Hungarian Air Force who had joined in the Battle of Stalingrad. Defiantly, Golubev led his *Shturmoviki* into the enemy formation, with guns blazing. In the brief encounter the Il-2 pilots shot two of the Messerschmitts from the skies.

The *Shturmoviki* pilots never let up throughout the war. Their tank destruction efforts became legend and they proved to be the deciding factor in many tank battles. The "Black Death" more than lived up to its name and reputation.

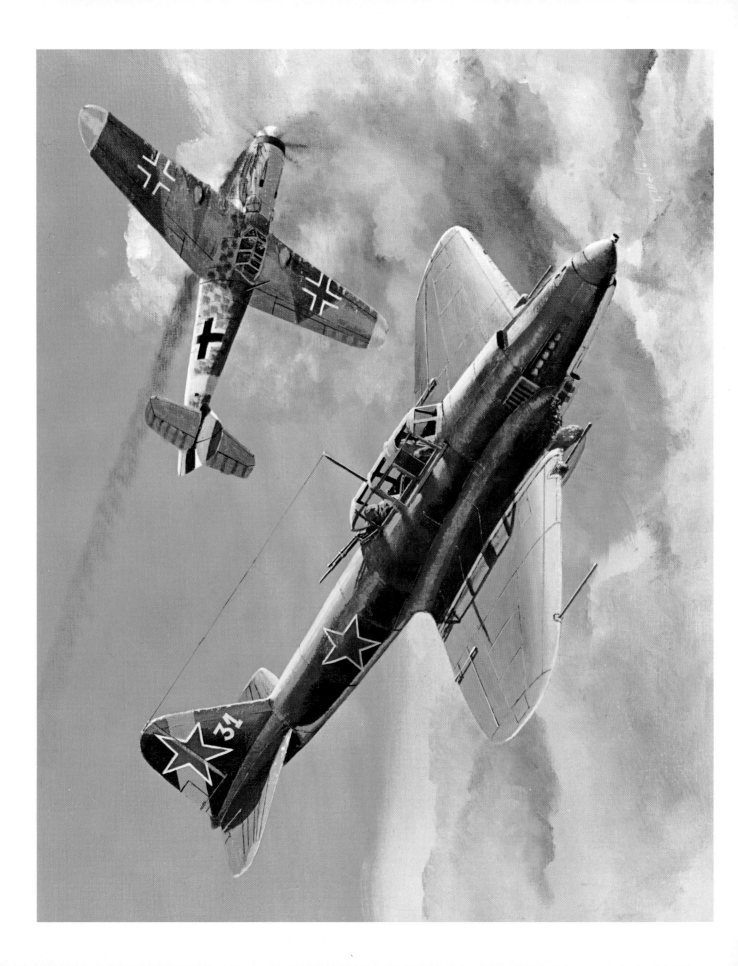

Fiat C.R. 42 *Falco*

The success of designer Ing. Celestino Rosatelli's biplane, the C.R. 32, during the Spanish Civil War no doubt inspired the Italian *Regia Aeronautica* to accept his model C.R. 42 for production in 1936. The C.R. 42 was the last of the biplane fighters to be put into production by any major power.

The Fiat fighter was not fast by World War II standards, with a maximum speed of 266 miles per hour at just above 13,000 feet, nor was it heavily armed, possessing only a pair of 12.7mm machine guns firing through the propeller. The C.R. 42 did, however, maneuver well, had excellent flying qualities, and was a sturdy and durable aircraft.

Several foreign countries took interest in the *Falco* during its early production. The Hungarians took delivery of a number of the fighters in 1939, the same year that the Italian *Regia Aeronautica* began to assign the first operational models to various *Stormo*.

The first C.R. 42's to see combat were those assigned to the 2 *eme Groupe de Chasse* in Belgium. When, on 10 May 1940, that country was attacked by the Germans, the majority of the assigned C.R. 42's were caught on the ground where they were destroyed by bombing and strafing. Before their final destruction, however, a few of them did get airborne and entered combat with the Germans, and obtained three victories.

When Italy entered World War II on 10 June 1940, the Fiat C.R. 42 was the newest type of fighter assigned to the *Regia Aeronautica*. They were committed to action on 12 June 1940, when *Falcos* of the 23rd and 151st *Gruppos* attacked French airfields at Hyeres and

Fayence where they destroyed some twenty aircraft on the ground and shot down one in aerial combat.

The C.R. 42 saw major action in both Italian East Africa and in the North African campaign. The *Falco* units were constantly in action against units of the Royal Air Force in both of these theaters as well as in the skies over Greece during the action in early 1941.

Classic amongst these actions were the last of the biplane dogfights. Depicted is a combat of renown that took place on 8 August 1940, between *Falcos* of the 9th and 10th *Gruppo*, 4th *Stormo* of the *Regia Aeronautica*, and No. 80 Squadron of the Royal Air Force which was flying Gloster *Gladiators*. Nine of the C.R. 42's were shot down while the Italians claimed five of the *Gladiators*.

In the course of the action, Sgt. Lido Poli, who was seriously wounded early in the fight, continued the combat until he had downed one of the opposing *Gladiators*. Poli then made a forced landing and was immediately taken to the hospital, where doctors found it necessary to amputate a wounded arm. Sgt. Poli was awarded the Medaglio d'Oro for his courageous action.

The C.R. 42 continued to see action throughout the North African campaign, then followed the action as it progressed to Sicily and then Italy. When the Italian government surrendered in 1943, a number of *Falcos* were flown to Germany, where they saw limited action in combat but considerable duty as a training aircraft up to the end of the war in 1945.

THE LUFTWAFFE GALLERY

Eagles in the Sky

Foreword

Luftwaffe! Why, the very sight and sound of the word has the ring of audacity and the promise of a daring force to be reckoned with!

One can only wonder what would be our current state of aviation in general, and war-readiness in particular, had a high state-of-the-art not been present in the Luftwaffe when the hostilities began. The awesome power of the German war machine, the Luftwaffe in particular, forced the Allied aircraft designers to be extremely inventive, and to do it in a hurry.

Luftwaffe planes, pilots, strategies, and tactics forced a giant step forward in aerial warfare. The pace was greatly quickened. No longer could designers think in terms of biplanes or even the small and zippy monoplanes. Neither would the .303-caliber machine guns, usually just a pair of them, pose much of a threat to these powerful new German aircraft. The Germans came at you lightning fast, their cannons clearing the skies in short order; they were eagles among outdated birds of prey.

German ingenuity outstripped all others to put the world's first jet racing in the sky, then the one and only rocket-powered plane to dive from high and flash through bomber formations to bewilder and confound the crews. V-1's and V-2's streaked across the Channel to rain down on southern England.

The names of Messerschmitt, Heinkel, and Junkers quickly became better known than those of twenty American presidents. Luftwaffe! *Blitzkrieg!* Schwarme and gaggle burst into the English language, to stay there even to this day.

A great air force, to be sure!

Here, then, are but twelve of these mighty air machines: Heinkels over London, wasp-nosed Bf 110's tearing up a Russian airfield, "Pip" Priller scattering *Lightnings,* the *Uhu* knocking down a *Mossie,* Bartels challenging the "Baby Air Force," and much, much more that will bring goosebumps to your flesh.

Eagles in the Sky is now a part of James Ross McDowell's private collection.

Fieseler Fi 156 *Storch*

The Fieseler Fi 156 *Storch* was probably the best all around observation and light reconnaissance aircraft of World War II. Its short takeoff and landing performance made it a superb aircraft for liaison and ambulance service.

When World War II began with the invasion of Poland in September of 1939, one of the first aircraft to fly reconnaissance missions ahead of the German Panzer forces was the Fieseler *Storch*. The aircraft saw yeoman duty during the *blitzkrieg* into France in 1940, and then went to North Africa with Rommel's legions. Its performance was legendary wherever it went and whatever the mission. Possession of the aircraft was a matter of position with German staff officers, and was a highly esteemed prize for Allied forces when they were able to capture one of the craft on the ground.

The flying weight of the *Storch* was only a little over 2,700 pounds, and its Argus eight-cylinder engine could propel the little craft along at a top speed of 165 m.p.h., but its normal cruise was only about 90 m.p.h. With a bit of head wind, and by utilizing its flaps, it could mush along at approximately 30 m.p.h., and, under certain conditions, it could become airborne in a scant 230 feet.

Its short takeoff and landing capability made the *Storch* a forerunner to the helicopter for transporting wounded from the battlefield. Many lives were saved by its ability to get into difficult terrain to perform these missions of mercy.

Following the invasion of Italy at Anzio on 22 January 1944, it was imperative for the U.S. Army Air Force to neutralize all Luftwaffe bases in the area. It was on just such a mission that the *Spitfires* of the

101

52nd Fighter Group encountered a small formation of German aircraft in the vicinity of Piombioa, Italy. Leading one squadron of the *Spitfires* was veteran Eagle Squadron pilot Lt. Richard L. "Dixie" Alexander.

Amongst the aircraft speeding away from the Luftwaffe field were two Fieseler *Storchs* towing little gliders. Alexander went down after one of the craft, whose pilot immediately cut the glider loose and then sped up to seek safety in a mountain pass. This highly maneuverable aircraft represented one of the hardest of all targets to hit, and "Dixie" Alexander knew it. He closed rapidly on the *Storch* and let fly with a burst while the German was in an evasive turn, and missed! Now "Dixie" pulled the nose of his *Spit* way 'round and gave the *Storch* a lot of deflection. The burst hit the little airplane in the tail section, and the *Storch* simply disintegrated.

Such occasions were very rare. Normally, fighter planes never got a chance to get a telling burst into the highly maneuverable craft. The few that were destroyed in combat were usually victims of ground fire.

To be sure, the many capabilities of the Fieseler *Storch* left an indelible mark in the annals of World War II.

Heinkel He 111

Hauptmann Albert Hufenreuter ignored the charts spread out in front of him. As navigator and aircraft commander of a Luftwaffe Heinkel He 111 medium bomber bound for England, he had flown over London, his target for tonight, many times before. Taking off from its base near Lille, in northern France, his He 111 was bearing northeast toward the English Channel. Soon the plane was lost in the murky black darkness of the night.

The date was 10 May 1941, and this was to be a maximum effort— "The final blow against London," according to the Nazi propaganda machine. All available aircraft of Luftwaffe West were to join in the attack on Britain's capital. Heading toward the chalk-white cliffs of Dover that delineated the English coast, were *Kampfgeschwadern* of Dorniers, twin-engined Bf 110's, and Heinkels, all flying at different assigned altitudes and with specifically allocated sectors to attack.

Prior to takeoff, at the briefing, the *staffel* leader had announced that following this mission the unit was being transferred to a new base, a great distance from Lille. He didn't say where—perhaps he didn't know yet himself. But this announcement served to add further apprehension to the mission.

Hauptmann Hufenreuter had mixed emotions about his aircraft. At times he loved the old Heinkel, and at other times he hated it. In recent missions she had brought him back safely from bombing runs against a British battleship under construction at Barrow-in-Furness, the Dumbarton shipyards in the Firth-of-Clyde, and, of course, from raids over London. She could cruise economically for up to nine hours at 300 kilometers per hour and was one of the safest planes Hufenreuter had ever flown. But in combat, it was another story. Her low speed and lack of maneuverability made the Heinkel easy prey for any fighter by day, and at night she was an even easier target for the night fighters.

The 111, which was powered by two 1,200 h.p. Junkers Jumo inverted V-type engines, had a range of 758 miles with a maximum bomb load of close to 2¼ tons. This range was far more than was

needed for the short cross-channel run from northern France to England, and it provided a healthy reserve. The He 111 had been a civil transport before the war and required the addition of a vertical gondola in which a 20mm cannon was housed. A total of five 7.9mm machine guns mounted in the nose, dorsal, ventral, and beam positions completed the armament. It got its baptism of fire as a combat aircraft in the *Kondor Legion*, during the Spanish Civil War.

Bearing northeast, Hufenreuter ordered the sergeant-pilot to gain altitude as quickly as possible. Climbing, they made a wide swing, heading for the narrowest crossing of the Channel, between Calais and Cape Gris-Nez on the French side and Dover and Folkestone in England. Because of the climbing, it took a half-hour to reach the Bristish coast, at an altitude of about 6,000 meters. Dead ahead the crew could see London lit up by the hundreds of blazing fires. Dropping to about 2,000 meters, they could easily make out the big docks, sheds, factories, and other large buildings along the Thames River.

This night the sky was a melee of aircraft, probing searchlight beams, bursts of ack-ack, parachute flares, bomb flashes, the rising smoke, and British night fighters streaking in and out of the bomber formations.

Hufenreuter released his bombs on target and while still over London, turned south toward the Channel and climbed steeply to 4,000 meters. Leaving that raging hell behind him, Hufenreuter warned his four-man crew, "Keep your eyes open, boys! We aren't out of it yet! Watch out for night fighters!"

His warning was not without substance. Within a matter of seconds he saw a burst of about a dozen tracer bullets whip by below the left wing. "Night fighters! Dive, dive!" he shouted. But it was too late. A second burst caught the port engine.

Hufenreuter never knew what hit his aircraft. It was probably a *Hurricane*, but he didn't see it. The Heinkel dived, took evasive action, and appeared to have lost the attacking fighter.

The instrument needles had gone haywire, and at 1,500 meters the port engine stopped completely. At an altitude of 1,000 meters they could see the silvery water of the Channel up ahead. But the trees and bushes were rushing up fast as the pilot shouted, "*Hauptmann*, I can't hold her...!"

Hauptmann Hufenreuter and his crew sat out the rest of the war in a British P.O.W. camp. Following V-E Day, he returned to Germany, where he became an English teacher.

Messerschmitt Bf 109-G *Gustav*

During the course of World War II, the Luftwaffe constantly modified and up-dated its first line fighter—the Messerschmitt Bf 109.

Upon the arrival of the *Spitfire* Mark V as an opponent, the Messerschmitt Bf 109-E gave way to the Bf 109-F, with its rounded wing tips, modified fuselage, and new engine. During the summer of 1943, the fighter units of the Luftwaffe began to take delivery of what was perhaps the most famous of the Messerschmitt Bf 109 line—the "G", or *Gustav*—most of which incorporated a new armament, and all of which were powered by a 1,475 horsepower Daimler-Benz engine. The new armament package consisted of the customary engine-mounted 20mm cannon firing through the propeller hub, but instead of the two 7.9mm machine guns firing through the propeller, it mounted two 13mm machine guns, which necessitated fairings on the gun breeches that gave the model its noticeable bulges just forward of the cockpit.

By late 1943 the *Gustav* was standard equipment for most of the *Geschwader* in the Luftwaffe. Amongst those based in the Mediterranean who were flying the craft was the IV/JG 27 at Kalamaki in Greece. A young German pilot, who wore the Knight's Cross, was assigned to the unit that summer. He was *Oberfeldwebel* Heinrich Bartels, and he had won the coveted Knight's Cross for downing 47 Russian aircraft on the Eastern Front.

Opposite the Luftwaffe forces in Greece was the "Baby Air Force" of the Mediterranean, which was composed of the B-25 medium bombers of the 12th Air Force's 321st Group, supported by the veteran P-38-equipped 82nd Fighter Group. The bombers were assigned targets in Greece, Yugoslavia, and Albania, as a rule, while the P-38's escorted them, giving battle to the Luftwaffe fighters and doing bombing and strafing work of their own.

On 15 November 1943, the *Mitchells* of the 321st Group set out to destroy the airbase at Kalamaki which was proving to be a real thorn in the side of the "Baby Air Force." As usual they were escorted by the P-38's of the 82nd Fighter Group. Over the target, they were attacked in force by the Messerschmitt *Gustavs* of IV/JG 27. In the heated air battle, *Obw.* Bartels downed one of the *Mitchell* bombers as well as one of the *Lightnings*. In the constant action of late 1943, Bartels would score some 20 victories while flying against the "Baby Air Force" and other units of the A.A.F. and R.A.F. operating in the Aegean area.

The pilots of the Luftwaffe continued to operate the Bf-G's until the end of the war. Many of the higher scoring aces of the Luftwaffe on the Eastern Front scored the majority of their successes flying the famed *Gustav*. Bartels would go on to score 99 victories in the craft before he was killed in action on 23 December 1944 while flying on the Western Front.

Henschel Hs 129

The Henschel Hs 129 had to overcome an "ugly duckling" reputation before it won fame in the Luftwaffe. Although it was originally designed as a ground support aircraft, the Hs 129 was far from an immediate success. In its original conformation the aircraft was underpowered, the pilot's view was restricted considerably, and flight performance was very poor.

The Luftwaffe refused to utilize facilities in Germany for modification, so the Hs 129 was refitted with captured French Gnome Rhone radial engines. This improved performance to some extent. The armament combinations carried by the aircraft were formidable, with two 7.9mm machine guns and two 20mm cannons for basics.

The aircraft saw its initial action in North Africa, where the Gnome Rhone engine was no match for the desert dust. After numerous engine failures the Hs 129's were pulled out of combat and sent to the rear for refitting with sand filters, but to no great avail.

In late 1942 the Hs 129's were sent to Russia, where they were to perform anti-tank duty, and it was here that the little twin-engined craft won its fame. During July of 1943, the Henschel Hs 129 wrought tremendous havoc upon Soviet tanks, and on one occasion repulsed an entire armored brigade. Operating in relays, four squadrons of Hs 129's destroyed most of the tanks during the concentrated attack.

As the war progressed, however, the Soviets developed new tanks which could not be stopped with the 20mm or, later, 30mm cannons that were used by the pilots of IV (Panzer) *Gruppe*/SG 9. It was found through experimentation that a 75mm gun could be used effectively when fired from the Hs 129. This electropneumatically operated gun was fitted on the aircraft and sent into action against the giant "Josef Stalin" tanks during the winter of 1944–45.

110

In January of 1945, one of the most outstanding tank destroyers of the Luftwaffe became Group Commander of I(PZ) SG 9. This was *Hauptmann* Andreas Kuffner, who had destroyed more than 50 tanks while flying the Hs 129. Kuffner continued his success and was the victor several times while using his 75mm cannon against the heavily armored "Josef Stalin" tank. Before his death in April of 1945, Kuffner had bagged in excess of 60 tanks.

The "ugly duckling" of the Luftwaffe had become the Panzer scourge of the Russian tank forces and left a record that is unparalleled in anti-tank warfare right to this day.

Focke Wulf Fw 190

Although it was not produced in the quantity of the Messerschmitt Bf 109, the Focke Wulf 190 absorbed the brunt of the action on the Western Front from early 1942 until the end of the war. Its big radial engine, clean lines, and heavy armament made the airplane an excellent choice to be operated in a number of roles. However, it was as an interceptor of the Allied bomber streams that the 190 gained its fame.

Beginning in the spring of 1942, the Focke Wulf 190 saw yeoman duty in the skies over France and the Channel coast, where it engaged in combat with the bombers and intruders of the Royal Air Force. When the American daylight bombardment campaign began that summer, it was the Focke Wulf 190 that made the interceptions and all but made the plan fail due to unacceptable losses to the bomber forces.

Once the heavy bombardment really got underway during daylight hours, the Focke Wulf 190's of JG 1 and JG 26 were fitted with rocket tubes to add to the existing firepower from the two machine guns and four 20mm cannons which were standard armament. On "Black Thursday," 14 October 1943, when the *Fortresses* went deep into Germany, to Schweinfurt, which was beyond the range of any fighter escorts at that time, it was the Focke Wulf 190's of these two units that rose to do battle and downed the majority of the sixty-two B-17's that failed to return from the mission.

However, the ever-increasing number of Allied fighters, and the advent of the P-51 *Mustang* as an escort fighter capable of going with the bombers to any target in Germany, began to take its toll on the small number of Luftwaffe fighters available in the West. Coupled with a heavy loss of experienced pilots in the East and the Mediterranean, the German Fighter Force did well to mount the attacks they did throughout the great air battles in the spring of 1944.

When D-Day in Normandy came on 6 June 1944, most of the Focke Wulfs had just moved from their bases on the Channel coast to bases further south to escape the constant pounding they were taking from both Allied bombers and fighters. So it happened that on D-Day only the *Kommodore* of JG 26, Major Josef "Pip" Priller, and his wingman were available to face the monstrous invasion. Undaunted, Priller and *FW.* Wodarczyk made a strafing run along the beach and then speedily and prudently left the scene.

Five days later Priller scored his 99th victory. The P-38 *Lightnings* of the 55th Fighter Group, under the command of Major Giller, were assigned to attack the German airfields and marshalling yards south of the invasion beaches. When the alarm came, Priller led his squadron of Focke Wulf 190's into the air to do battle with the Americans. Contact was made in the vicinity of Ressons, where a heated air battle immediately took place between ten Focke Wulf 190's of JG 26 and ten to twelve P-38's of the 55th Fighter Group.

Priller dived down and immediately slid in on the tail of one of the *Lightnings.* A burst from his cannon set the aircraft aflame and it went down. Lt. Gerd Wiegand scored telling hits on another one of the *Lightnings*, then watched as the pilot bailed out when the craft's engine burst into flames. Two of the P-38's were downed and several others suffered heavy damage, while three of the Fw 190's failed to return to base.

Four days later Priller scored his 100th victory, for which he was awarded the Oak Leaves with Swords to the Knight's Cross. This great German fighter pilot was to score only once more: a P-51 *Mustang* on 12 October 1944. Priller's 101 victories were all scored on the Western Front and, miraculously, he was never shot down in all his years of air combat.

The Focke Wulf 190 continued to see constant combat right up to the end of the war. Its later version, which incorporated the Junkers Jumo in-line engine, was one of the finest fighter planes to see action during the World War II era. The long-nosed 190 took a heavy toll of Allied bombers and fighters alike before the hostilities ceased in May of 1945.

Messerschmitt Me 410

Throughout World War II the Germans attempted to come up with a real destroyer-type aircraft that could wreak heavy destruction on the American bomber formations. The Messerschmitt Me 210 was one of the aircraft built specifically to deal with the problem. As a bomber-destroyer, it possessed heavy armament in the nose section, with two 20mm cannons and two 7.9mm machine guns. The plane also carried two remote-controlled rearward-firing 13mm machine guns that were mounted on barbettes attached to the sides of the fuselage. The aircraft's speed of 385 m.p.h. was good and the approximately 1,500-mile range was satisfactory. But, alas, it was loaded with "bugs." The plane suffered from all of the different ailments known to plague combat-type aircraft, and its accident rate was appalling. In short, the 210 was a dismal failure.

Then, in 1943, its successor made its appearance. This was the Messerschmitt Me 410, which was basically the Me 210 with a new engine. The bug-riddled plane's performance improved immediately with installation of the new engine, and in late 1943 and early 1944 the Me 410 began operating successfully as a fighter-bomber over the British Isles, where it became a formidable opponent to the R.A.F.'s *Mosquito* night fighter.

The Luftwaffe, however, still needed a good bomber-destroyer to carry a heavy weapon that could take to task the American daylight bombers, yet could remain out of range of the .50-caliber machine guns of the *Fortresses* and *Liberators*. In early 1944, German technicians began experimenting with the use of the BK 50mm cannon in the nose section of the Messerschmitt Me 410. This installation proved to be so successful that a number of Me 410A-2's on the production line were modified to utilize the weapon.

Accordingly, the cannon-armed Me 410 was supplied in good numbers to II/ZG 26 for home defense against the heavy bomber formations. Initially, the unit scored numerous successes with the heavy weapon. Approaching the bomber formation from abeam, the Me 410 pilots would commence blasting away with the deadly cannon while standing well out of range of the bomber's guns. Losses were few, while damage to the helpless bombers was great.

II/ZG 26's luck ran out, however, on 13 May 1944. On this day B-17's of the 8th Air Force's 96th Bombardment Group came under a savage attack by the Me 410's until P-51's of the 335th Fighter Group arrived on the scene. The *Mustangs* raced into the sluggish Me 410's and broke up the attack immediately, blasting six of the 410's from the sky in quick order. As the Messerschmitts fled from the melee they were jumped again, this time by P-51's of the 357th Fighter Group, which further decimated the ranks. II/ZG 26 suffered such heavy casualties that they never again took their 410's into action against the bombers.

The Messerschmitt Me 410 did, however, continue to operate in the various theaters of Europe until the end of the war, but never again did it enjoy any degree of success as a destroyer of American bomber formations.

◀ *Messerschmitt Me 410*

Messerschmitt Me 262

Throughout the early years of World War II, Adolf Hitler boasted of the German "secret weapons" that would change the complexion of warfare. How ironic it was that his decree to make the Messerschmitt Me 262—one of his vaunted "secret weapons"—a bomber, rather than a fighter, probably prevented the Allies from losing air superiority over Europe!

The Me 262 first flew on 18 July 1942, and while not the first German jet to fly, it was by far the most superior. Many mechanical and engineering problems held up early production of the Junkers Jumo jet-propelled aircraft, but by late 1943 four prototypes had been built and it was decided the time had come to demonstrate the Me 262 to Hitler, in the hope that he would order it into mass production.

When the jet flew for Hitler at Insterburg on 26 November 1943, he was greatly impressed, but he acclaimed the aircraft to be a high speed bomber. From that day forward any production of the Me 262 that was directed toward fighter operations had to be handled very discreetly.

The Me 262 went operational with a test group in September of 1944, and these crafts were transferred to *Kommando Nowotny*, which was led by the high scoring Luftwaffe ace, Major Walter Nowotny. This group met with limited success in combat and was disbanded after the loss of their leader on 8 November 1944.

As a bomber, the Me 262 did go into service in the fall of 1944, but, due to its speed and the limited bomb load, its missions could only be described as nuisance raids.

Fighter Forces organized the jet-propelled force into *Jagdgeschwader 7 Nowotny* in late 1944 and the unit scored its first victory on 26 December 1944. With experienced pilots at the controls, the four 30mm cannon-armed crafts were quite effective in high speed passes against Allied bombers, but it was felt that they could be made much more deadly if rockets were also used. After considerable experimentation, a number of Me 262's began utilizing as many as twenty-four 55mm R4M rockets, which were mounted on rails under the wings.

JG 7 met with considerable success despite great odds and operational difficulties. The Allies had no fighter plane that was capable of catching the Me 262, and the German pilots could avoid combat with the bomber escorts at will. The Allies, however, held air superiority and their fighters chose to orbit the Luftwaffe jet bases where they could attack the Me 262's during takeoffs and landings. Even when the Luftwaffe used Messerschmitt Bf 109's and Focke Wulf Fw 190's to protect the bases, the strategy didn't prove to be too effective in deterring the tenacious Allied fighters. Once in the air, however, the Me 262 performed brilliantly. By the end of the war, JG 7 alone had claimed some 400 victories, with 300 of them being four-engined Allied bombers.

In January of 1945, the most celebrated fighter unit of WW II was formed. General Adolf Galland, Commander of the German Fighter Forces, had fallen from grace with the Nazi High Command and was relegated to combat duty. Galland formed *Jagdverband* (JV) 44, an elite unit of veteran fighter pilots. Of the 50 pilots assigned to JV 44, ten were holders of the coveted Knight's Cross.

JV 44 operated in flights of three aircraft during combat. Upon sighting a formation of Allied bombers they would form-up high and to the rear. As they dove down in a high-speed pass, they would first fire their rockets and then follow up with 30mm cannon fire. Once the pass had been completed, they would go into a high-speed flat climbing turn just over the bomber formation. At this speed it was most difficult for the gunners in the bombers to track rapidly enough to hit them.

One of the more actively concentrated days of attack by the Me 262's against the Allied bomber formations was 7 April 1945. Fifteen American heavy bombers were lost that day, most of them to the German jets. One of the B-24 formations attacked was that of the 8th Air Force's 734th Squadron of the 453rd Bomb Group. As the gunners blazed away, the Me 262's of JV 44 dived down in a defiant pass. Two of the bombers fell away in flames, but one of the attackers went down trailing heavy smoke. The jets could be hit!

But for Hitler's order to make it be a bomber, many more American bombers would have fallen to the rockets and guns of the world's first jet-propelled fighter.

Focke Wulf Fw 200 *Condor*

"The Focke Wulf and other bombers employed against our shipping must be attacked in the air and in their nests!" was the order Winston Churchill gave to his fighting forces on 6 March 1941. It was, however, too late to save the *Empress of Britain*.

On 27 May 1931, one of the most magnificent ships of her day slid down the ways at Southampton. The Prince of Wales—later, King Edward VIII—did the honors by smashing a bottle of champagne against the bow of the second *Empress of Britain*. On her maiden voyage, she carried Mary Pickford and Douglas Fairbanks among her distinguished passengers. She was the largest and most luxurious vessel put into service by the Canadian Pacific Line up to that time. The 42,000 ton *Empress* was the first ocean liner equipped with ship-to-shore radio-telephone. Among her many other features were a full-size doubles tennis court, squash court, indoor Olympic swimming pool as well as a smaller open deck pool, a fully equipped gym, Turkish baths, and more. Like the *QE II* and *Rotterdam* of today, she sailed on round-the-world cruises. The *Empress* was truly a magnificent ship.

In July 1937, Kurt Tank, who was shortly to design the great German fighter plane—the Fw 190—sat at the controls of his new 26-passenger airliner on her first flight. He was pleased with the results of his engineering skill. The four-engined Focke Wulf 200 *Condor* also performed spectacularly in flights from Berlin to New York and return, and from Berlin to Tokyo.

Like the Dornier Do 17 and the Heinkel He 111, the *Condor* originally entered service as a civilian transport plane for *Deutsche Lufthansa*. Designing civilian aircraft, with the military mission in mind, was a ruse employed by the Nazis to get around the Treaty of Versailles that prohibited Germany from re-arming. The treaty, which had ended World War I, sought to prevent Germany from ever again becoming a threat. Obviously, it failed.

In 1939, the *Empress* and the *Condor* received new assignments. They both went to war. The ocean liner was converted to a troopship and the airliner became a bomber.

In Germany, Luftwaffe *Oberst Leutnant* (Lt. Colonel) Edgar Peterson was ordered to select a suitable long-range maritime patrol bomber and to organize a *staffel*. He picked the *Condor*.

The Fw 200 first saw action carrying supplies to an isolated garrison during the Norwegian campaign. Its principal mission, however, was to seek out and destroy British shipping. Organized on 1 October 1939, Peterson's outfit was designated the First *Staffel* of *Kampfgeschwader* 40, or KG 40, early in 1940. By July of that year the *staffel* was increased to the strength of a group, and later another group was added. All of KG 40's *Condors* bore the unit's "World-in-a-Ring" insignia slightly aft of the pilot's compartment on both sides, and each had the name of a different star or planet across its nose.

On 26 October 1940, the *Empress of Britain* met a Fw 200 *Condor* seventy miles off the northwest coast of Ireland. *Hauptmann* (Captain) Bernhard Jope was on his first mission with KG 40 when he spotted the troopship. The *Empress* had few, if any, air defenses, and Jope brought his Fw 200 in very low over the water. The *Condor's* bomb sight was not effective at low altitude, but the bomb release was rigged to drop the five 550-pound bombs at eight yard intervals. Two of them struck home, leaving the once proud *Empress* crippled and on fire. Two days later, while being towed by a Polish destroyer, she was torpedoed and sunk by the German submarine U-32.

The tactics employed by Jope were used effectively by the rest of the *geschwader*, and during the first quarter of 1941 the *Condors* sank 88 ships for a total of 390,000 tons. This was accomplished by no more than eight Fw 200's, the maximum KG 40 could muster at any one time.

No fools the British, they soon armed their merchant ships and the picnic was over.

Heinkel He 219 *Uhu*

Only two aircraft that had been designed from the ground up as night fighters saw action during World War II. These were the Heinkel 219 *Uhu* (Owl) of the Luftwaffe and Northrop's P-61 *Black Widow* of the U.S.A.A.F. The excellent Bf 110 *Zerstörer* was, like the R.A.F.'s *Mosquito*, an adaptation of an existing design and not a purposely built night fighter.

Design work on both of these night fighters began in 1940 and, as it turned out, each were to be relatively large, twin-engined machines. Production of the *Uhu* was slow and limited, hence the number on hand at any given time was not very large. This was due to the fact that day fighters and more established aircraft were given priority position on the assembly line. Although the *Uhu* was much heavier than the *Black Widow*, it achieved a higher top speed, greater altitude, longer range, and carried a heavier armament package on slightly less powerful engines. The *Black Widow* did, however, possess the better radar equipment. On the other hand, *Uhu* possessed a very special innovation—it was the first major service type to feature ejection seats for its crew.

The Heinkel claimed its first victories a full year before the *Black Widow*. Neither plane was used on a wide-scale basis until in the latter part of 1944. And the German night fighter emerged as the better performer of the two.

Carrying both forward-firing guns and the upward-firing *Schrage Musik* (the literal translation is "slanting music," but is, in fact, the German term for "Jazz") installation, the He 219 was capable of inflicting untold havoc on a bomber stream. During the first

operational sortie with a pre-production test aircraft, the Luftwaffe's leading night fighter pilot of the period, Major Werner Streib, claimed five bombers shot down during the night of 11/12 June 1943. During the first six sorties made by He 219's in the summer of 1943, twenty British aircraft fell victim to the *Uhu's* guns, including no less than six *Mosquitos*. Indeed, the aircraft proved to be the only German night fighter in service prior to 1945 that had any real chance of catching or combatting the various versions of the formidable *Mosquito*, which at the time was operating virtually unmolested over Germany as a bomber, photo-reconnaissance aircraft, and intruder fighter, and increasingly as a night counter-air and escort fighter.

Our scene depicts an He 219 *Uhu* of 1/*Nachtjagdgeschwader* 1, the main unit employing these aircraft, scorching a *Mossie*, its most difficult quarry.

Messerschmitt Me 163 *Komet*

Although 8th Air Force commanders had known for some time that the German Luftwaffe was readying jet- and rocket-powered aircraft, it was not until July of 1944 that this menace made its formal appearance in the skies. Colonel Avelin Tacon, C.O. of the 359th Fighter Group, reported sighting, and attempting to combat, two of the rocket-powered Messerschmitt Me 163's on 28 July 1944.

All 8th Air Force units took notice of the report and readied themselves for possible attacks. The following day, Captain Arthur Jeffrey, of the 479th Fighter Group, encountered one of the speedy craft and managed to put some shots into it before he lost the *Komet* in a 500 m.p.h. dive.

By August of 1944, I/JG 400, the unit equipped with the Me 163, was based at Brandis, near Leipzig, Germany. It was hoped that from here the interceptors would be effective in driving the American bombers from the industrial plants in the area.

When on 16 August 1944 the heavy bombers of the 8th Air Force attacked targets in this area, the Luftwaffe intercepted them in strength. A B-17 *Flying Fortress* named "Outhouse Mouse" from the 91st Bombardment Group was one of the bombers to encounter the full force of the German attackers. First, "Outhouse Mouse" was knocked out of formation by a Fw 190 and a Messerschmitt 109, both of which inflicted material damage to the bomber and wounded two of its crew members.

Then, as it limped along, it came under attack from a flight of two of the Messerschmitt Me 163 *Komets*. The German pilot brought his rocketing fighter down in a screaming dive, aiming on the tail of

"Outhouse Mouse," while Lt. Reese Mullins took every kind of evasive action he knew in the attempt to escape the attacker's cannon fire. And Mullins was apparently effective, for the Me 163 pilot couldn't seem to get his guns lined up on the B-17.

Simultaneous with the German's attack, Lt. Colonel John B. Murphy and Lt. Cyril W. Jones of the 359th Fighter Group spotted the Me 163's going after the crippled *Fortress* and came roaring down to give assistance. There was no way they could catch the German in his dive, but after the *Komet* came out of the dive, Murphy caught him, got in a short burst, and then overran the craft. Lt. Jones caught the Me 163 as it rolled over and put a good burst into it, but then blacked out when he tried to follow it through on its dive.

Murphy then caught another Me 163 making shallow diving turns at a lower altitude. It could have been that the 8 to 12 minute fuel supply had been expended by the German pilot. Regardless, Murphy rapidly overtook him and scored hits on the fighter until a violent explosion occurred; the disintegrating *Komet* continued its downward plunge, streaming fire and parts all the way to the ground.

Although it attracted a lot of attention, the Messerschmitt Me 163 was never a combat success. Very few Allied aircraft were downed by it, while many of the German pilots fell victim to the erratic performance of their own aircraft.

Junkers Ju 88

The Junkers Ju 88 was probably the most versatile twin-engined aircraft utilized by the Luftwaffe in World War II. It was a medium altitude bomber, a dive bomber, a daylight fighter against the Allied bomber streams, and a long-range night intruder or interceptor, as the case might be.

The initial unit to take the Junkers Ju 88 into combat was KG 30, which struck the British Fleet in the Firth-of-Forth on 26 September 1939. KG 30 served with distinction throughout the Battle of France, the Battle of Britain, and took part in the initial onslaught on Russia.

Spring of 1942 saw the Allies trying desperately to get supplies to Russia across the North Atlantic. Slowly, but surely, progress was being made in the anti-submarine campaign, and, as the result, the German U-boat concentrations were being pushed further and further eastward. The wolf packs of U-boats and long-range German aircraft were, however, still taking their toll of the merchant vessels steaming in convoys bound for the Russian port of Murmansk.

One of the Luftwaffe units that was striking against the convoys from its base in Norway was III *Gruppe* of the famed KG 30. Among the veteran pilots assigned to III/KG 30 at that time was Major Werner Baumbach, who would win the Knight's Cross with Swords for his efforts against the convoys. Baumbach had seen extensive action since the beginning of the war and both he and his crew knew no peers when it came to anti-shipping strikes.

On a sunny Sunday afternoon in the spring of 1942, Baumbach lifted his Ju 88 from the runway of the airfield at Stavanger-Sola in Norway and climbed steadily as he took a westward course. Long-

range reconnaissance aircraft had reported Allied supply vessels were docked in the Danish-owned Faeroe Islands, which lay in the North Atlantic between Scotland's Shetland Islands and Iceland. Baumbach and his Ju 88 crew had been waiting for a break in the weather to strike at these vessels, and today was the day.

The course to the Faeroe Islands took the Ju 88 far out to sea, nearly 375 miles from their home base. After an uneventful flight, the jagged, rocky summits of the islands made their appearance above the clouds. Baumbach maneuvered the Junkers around to come in the target area from the west. The clouds seemed to part in the target area, and the Junkers came roaring in over Thornshavn fjord. There before Baumbach was a large merchant vessel, with several smaller ships behind it, sitting out in open waters.

Baumbach nosed the Junkers over in a diving attack and swiftly closed the distance to the target. Quickly, he lined up on the big ship as its decks grew larger and larger in his sights. Then, a push of the button and the bombs were away. The first projectile fell short, but the second scored a direct hit on the port side of the ship. Black clouds of smoke rose from the target as Baumbach set the Junkers on a course for the long flight home.

The following day a reconnaissance plane reported that the ship was burned out and listing badly. Major Werner Baumbach had added another victim to his growing list of Allied ships sent to the bottom. Sixteen ships would feel the wrath of his strikes before he was promoted to command the German bomber forces for the balance of World War II.

Messerschmitt Bf 110 *Zerstörer*

The new Bf 110 *Zerstörer* (destroyer) was just entering service when the outbreak of World War II came in September of 1939. The aircraft had fired the enthusiasm of the Luftwaffe Commander-in-Chief, Hermann Göering, and the units flying *Zerstörers* were the "apple of his eye."

The *Zerstörergruppen* achieved notable successes when faced with low-performance adversaries, or unescorted bombers, over Poland, France, and the Low Countries, and over the North Sea and Norway. But when challenged by *Hurricanes* and *Spits* over Dunkirk, *Zerstörer* pilots suffered their first major setback, and the losses were heavy: The plane was unable to maneuver effectively against these British fighters. Moreover, the *Zerstörer* proved to be a dismal failure as a long-range escort for the Luftwaffe's bombers. In this role their losses bordered on being catastrophic; hence, the bombers, for all practical purposes, went unescorted. In the end, the *Zerstörers* had to have their own escorts of Bf 109's!

Events during the winter of '41, however, caused the Bf 110 to be tried out in the role of a night fighter. This was brought about by the ever increasing night raids by British bombers. Because the aircraft was a heavily armed, stable gun platform, the Bf 110 was an excellent bomber-destroyer and, as such, racked up many successes at night. As a result, the aircraft remained one of the numerically important types in the Luftwaffe's night defense force for the remainder of the war.

Campaigns in the Balkans and the North African Desert provided the means to give another role, and a new chance, to the

133

Zerstörergruppen still operating by day. They were employed down on the deck for ground attack missions, and the results were good, particularly when they went after an airfield. These successes took four *Gruppen* of Bf 110's to Russia when that country was invaded in 1941, and it was on this front where the *Zerstörer* amassed a legion of successes both as a day fighter and destroyer of ground targets. This was due primarily to the initial low quality of the opposition. In time this shortcoming of the Russians would change, but for the moment the *Gruppens* ran amuck, destroying hundreds and hundreds of Russian aircraft both in the sky and on the ground, laying waste to great numbers of tanks, trucks, gun emplacements, rail locomotives and rolling stock, and other such targets.

Our scene shows Bf 110's of II/ZG 1, the *Wespengruppe* (Wasp group), attacking Russian fighters caught napping on the ground in southern Russia.

All *Zestörergruppen* were subsequently withdrawn from Russia and returned to Germany, once again to go up as bomber destroyers to help counter the growing numbers of the 8th Air Force's B-17's and B-24's appearing over the *Reich*. Initially, the heavily armed and rugged Bf 110 proved extremely efficient at this task. Their destructive powers were short-lived, however, for with the appearance of long-range fighter escorts, coming with the bombers to targets deep inside Germany, the Bf 110's suffered terrible losses and were quickly driven from the skies.

The Original Canvases

Quite often it is asked: "What happens to the original paintings? Where can they be seen, if at all?" Well, I can promise you there is no way for the average person living in an average apartment or home to begin to hang some 75 large canvases. After the paintings have been faithfully recorded through the photographic process, they are transferred to new hands possessing the means to display them properly. Actually, the arrangements for the transfer are usually made well in advance of completing a gallery.

Over the years, air enthusiasts around the world have been privy to the work and closely follow its progress. From out of these aficionados there emerge those who have the desire and wherewithal to collect these truly magnificent paintings, and it is to them that we look to place the works. Because the subject of the originals is historical in nature, and is definitive and hence very expensive to produce, the canvases are released in "galleries" rather than one or two at a time. This precludes an initial scattering of the canvases and tends to cause them to be kept intact, which is necessary if they are ever to be seen by the interested public.

To date, sixty of the paintings are in the private collection of Mr. Douglas Champlin of Enid, Oklahoma. More outstanding than the paintings is Doug's excellent collection of real fighter plane types that saw combat duty during both World Wars. Doug has recently opened the doors of the Falcon Field Fighters Air Museum located in Mesa, Arizona, and it is here where the public can see both these famous fighter planes and the canvases. The Falcon Field Fighters is a definitive project inasmuch as it chronicles the development of the single-engine fighter from the beginning of World War I through the end of World War II. When the project is fully completed, the hangars at Falcon Field will have on display some 25 to 30 aircraft ranging from the Fokker and Sopwith through the Corsair and Focke Wulf. And all of them will have been completely restored to flying condition. So, if you are ever in the Phoenix area and want to witness a thrilling sight, stop by Falcon Field to catch both the fighters and the paintings.

Twelve originals—*The Luftwaffe Gallery*—are part of a private collection owned by Mr. James Ross McDowell, a Canadian businessman from Calgary, Alberta, who now resides in Scottsdale, Arizona. At the time this was written, Jim had no definite plan for where his originals will first appear on public display.

Other originals, commissioned by the 58th Bomb Wing Association, hang in the U.S. Naval Academy at Annapolis, Maryland; U.S. Military Academy at West Point, New York; U.S. Air Force Academy at Colorado Springs, Colorado; and the Admiral Nimitz Center in Fredericksburg, Texas. All of these paintings represent historical events in which the Boeing B-29 *Superfortress* was involved, along with the branch of service that received the original.

As fate would have it, not a single canvas has ended up with the Confederate Air Force, the organization that provided the inspiration for their creation!

Glenn Bavousett—coordinator

Les Bavousett—photographer

Ed Robertson—modeler

Donovan Gatewood—tracing artist

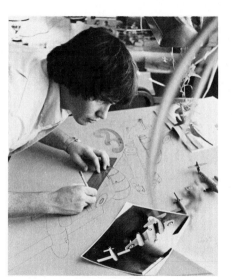

W.T. Wedell—color artist

The Team

Early on it was realized that time was the enemy in regard to adding to the pictorial documentation of the World War II era of our aviation history. By the mid-1970's, most of the people involved in the WW II air war were in their 50's or older. They were then, and still are now, disappearing at an alarming rate, and with them goes the means of experienced critiques necessary to help perfect the record.

Much more than what meets the eye is involved in creating a single scene. One person, working alone, performing all of the many chores to develop a scene, is severely handicapped and his or her rate of output is automatically restricted. In order to capture on canvas as many combat scenes as possible, and do it in the least amount of time, it was readily apparent that a team effort would be required to cope with this element of urgency.

Accordingly, the overall workload was analyzed to compartmentalize it into the various specialty areas. Then, someone was brought in with the talent and/or skill to handle each area. From this exercise was born the Glenn Illustrators team. This team concept permitted each of the team members to focus their full attention on their area of responsibility; hence, a greater rate of output was achieved and the end product came out better than initially expected. It was realized there would be no appreciable savings in the total time required to complete a scene. However, by dividing the time among the several functions, causing an overlapping, the actual calendar time required to complete a scene was shortened drastically. This was our way of fighting the clock.

My role in the effort was threefold: finance, coordinate, and set each scene. As the stories of the actions were assembled, it was my job to freeze a moment of each action for portrayal. Concurrent with this came the technical research for the markings, colors, etc., on the aircraft to be depicted. After all information had been gained, the scene was ready to be developed. Plastic model kits were acquired and the photographer was turned loose.

The photographer's first job was to go to the aircraft, if one existed, and take all of the shots necessary to give us the details. You cannot always trust the models, and most pictures in books and magazines are too small to do any good. Something is always lacking, so the best thing to do is find the real airplane and photograph it from nose to tail. This task carried Les all over this country as well as into Europe.

While Les was busy with the 35mm, our award-winning modeler, Ed Robertson, constructed the models, correcting all known flaws incorporated by the manufacturer. It is interesting to note that we do not apply any paint schemes or camouflage patterns on the models. Ed gives each a light gray spray job overall. Through trial and error we found this produced the best results when working with the black and white film which we used. Ed does, however, use a black ink pen to outline the camouflage pattern before all markings are fixed in place.

Next came Les' second job: Photographing the models. This was done in one of two ways, depending on the nature of the scene still locked in my mind: Suspending the models on thread or simply placing them on a dark table top to get contrast in color. In either instance Les photographed them from various camera angles, most of which were minute adjustments after I had looked through the lens to make sure the view closely matched the one in my mind's eye. We never were conservative when shooting the models. Too many shots were always better than too few. Les has his own darkroom, and therefore all filming costs are minimized.

Now we moved into the darkroom to develop the film, then fed it into the enlarger to search through the frames to find the one or ones that best presented the plane for the action. Eight by ten inch prints were made of these candidates. One by one they were positioned on the image board so the shots of the secondary aircraft to appear in the scene (if any) could be imaged on the print. This always resulted in much enlarging and reducing to find the proper size of the secondary aircraft for the scene. Then prints of secondary planes were made.

The developing scene now moved to my drawing board, where I laid out every piece of information obtained on the planes to be depicted, including the models and all photographs Les had acquired, as well as all of the books in my library that in any way covered these particular planes. Frosted acetate was placed over the 8 x 10 of the primary aircraft and it was then traced using a fine-pointed 2B lead pencil. Then the other planes were added in. At this point, no attempt was made to draw in the background for the scene.

The entire package now went to our tracing artist, Donovan Gatewood. The first thing Donovan does is to mechanically enlarge the 8 x 10 to canvas size, and we work to two standard sizes, both of which are proportional to 8 x 10: 24 x 30 inches for single-engine aircraft and 32 x 40 inches for multi-engine aircraft. After tracing the enlargement onto the canvas, Donovan then adds in the details not possible on the small pencil drawing. You may wonder why we bother with the small drawing. Well, it is ten times easier to work out the problems of setting the scene at that size than it is on the larger. Anyhow, Donovan's task was to clean up the scene and give the color artist as much detail as possible but, again, no background.

Now the scene was ready to be brought to life with color. The package was shifted to Tony's studio where he commenced work only after making a thorough study of the story and all supporting information. If the action called for a background showing land—such as in the *Kingcobra* scene—then it would be included in the package and already be enlarged to canvas size. Tony prefers to work up his own backgrounds. If the action was a sky scene—such as the Fw 190—then Tony was left to his imagination. Sometimes the research did reveal, more or less, what the weather was like at the time the action occurred. When it did not, and when it was possible to do so, the pilot or a crew member was contacted to see if he remembered. Some did, some did not. In any event, we usually knew the time of the year it happened and the hour of the day. From this information Tony at least had some idea of how to paint the sky. When we didn't know, or it simply did not matter, he incorporated a good old Texas sky.

After he saw in his artistic mind's eye how the scene was to look, Tony would begin working up the color. First, the entire scene was painted in grays, then the planes were masked out and the background completed in color. After the background was completed, the planes were unmasked and color applied following the gray tonal patterns.

Upon completing a canvas, it was taken to Meisel Photochrome in Dallas to acquire an 8 x 10 color transparency, two 4 x 5 copy negs, and several 8 x 10 color, borderless check-prints which were sent to the pilot and/or any other substantive sources of original input for critique purposes. When everyone was satisfied that the scene was an acceptable portrayal of the action, it was declared to be finished.

Through the combined efforts and talents of these individuals it was possible to cause things to happen in a minimum of time. It's a fine team and I am proud to have worked with each of them.

Index